EDGE
OF THE
UNKNOWN

BOSSINEY BOOKS

First published in 1995 by Bossiney Books,
St Teath, Bodmin, Cornwall.
Typeset and printed by Penwell Ltd, Callington, Cornwall.

ISBN 0 948158 99 9

ACKNOWLEDGEMENTS

Front cover: Roy Westlake
Front cover design: Maggie Ginger
Back cover: Ray Bishop
Photographs Ray Bishop
Drawings: Felicity Young

IT IS an interesting psychic fact that peaceful country lanes suddenly become the setting of ghostly manifestation. Sometimes in the form of sounds – footsteps or hoofbeats – or visible forms of people or animals and occasionally motor cars. Phantom coaches and horses are becoming things of the past: only very rare sightings. Is their disappearance tied up with the passage of time?

About the Author – and the book

MICHAEL WILLIAMS, a Cornishman, started full-time publishing in 1975. He and his wife Sonia live in a cottage on the shoulder of a green valley outside St Teath in North Cornwall.

His recent publications include **Psychic Phenomena of the West** and his highly acclaimed **Supernatural Search in Cornwall** has been reprinted. He is currently collaborating with Sarah Foot on Magical Places.

Outside his Bossiney activities, Michael Williams is a writing and publishing consultant, evaluating manuscripts and advising writers on their publishing prospects.

In addition to publishing and writing, Michael Williams is a keen cricketer and collector of cricket books and autographs. He was the first captain of the Cornish Crusaders Cricket Club and is today President of the Crusaders. He is also a member of Cornwall and Gloucestershire County Cricket Clubs – and a Vice-President of the Cornwall Rugby Football Union. A member of the International League for the Protection of Horses and the RSPCA, he has worked hard for reform in laws relating to animal welfare.

A member of the Ghost Club Society, he has a special interest in the paranormal. In **Edge of the Unknown**, Bossiney's 229th title, he investigates a wide range of cases in the Westcountry – many appearing in book form for the first time – and covers subjects as different as ghosts and the Holy Grail, atmosphere and time, supernatural literature and mysteries.

Author's Acknowledgements

I AM deeply indebted to various people who have given me interviews for this book and authors who have allowed me to quote from their works. In this, our 229th Bossiney title, I also thank Angela Larcombe for her thoughtful editing and Sally Dodd for her immaculate typing and perceptive comments. Last, but not least, I am grateful to Felicity Young for her drawings and Ray Bishop for his photographs; between them they must have produced more paranormal illustrations over the years than any other two people in British publishing.

AT THE EDGE OF THE UNKNOWN

WHEN we travel to the Edge of the Unknown we soon discover Britain is a very mysterious place, and here in the Westcountry we live in probably the most mysterious region of all.

In the Wellington area of Somerset various people have observed a phantom hitch-hiker on the A38. A reader from Wiltshire has asked me if I have any thoughts about a block of pink ice which crashed through a roof there in March 1985.

In Devon mysterious footprints in the snow have been attributed to the Devil. Yesterday I was told of a ghost currently haunting a property on Bodmin Moor. At the weekend I am scheduled to receive a letter which may throw some light on a mysterious event near Bristol. Last week the President of the Ghost Club Society asked me if I could do something to help a lady whose house in Cornwall is the target of a poltergeist activity. This afternoon I have been discussing with a fellow writer why Lawrence of Arabia's death at Cloud's Hill remains a Dorset mystery. Some supernatural happenings belong to history; others are taking place around us today.

These are challenging exciting times in the field of the paranormal, and I believe greater days lie ahead. The twenty-first century may well produce two important goals: first, proof of the reality of psychic phenomena; secondly, and just as important, we may discover ways and means of harnessing the supernatural and employing the enormous untapped forces inside us.

Only men and women with shut minds and shut eyes would decline to accept that strange forces are already at work: influences over which we have no control, and about which we have relatively

DESPITE the peaceful atmosphere of Dorset, you often feel in touch with a distant past. The Nine Stones at Winterbourne Abbas is such a place. Though cars hurry by on the road alongside, those railings seem symbolic, somehow dividing the here and now and the long ago. This small stone circle, 25 feet in diameter, was constructed in the Bronze Age and 'used for religious purposes.' I remember making my first visits to Dorset with keen anticipation. I had met Lady Clara Vyvyan, then living down on the lovely Lizard peninsula in South Cornwall; a truly great travel writer, she told me she rated a week's walking in Dorset a memorable exploration: 'I walked on into unknown country . . .' Here in Dorset you find a county thickly populated by ghosts. Almost every village and hamlet has at least one phantom, and they are not all silent characters. The anguished cries of a long dead smuggler have been heard at Westbarrow Bay, and at Purse Caundle Manor near Sherborne accounts of the chanting of plainsong – unaccompanied vocal music used in the Medieval Church.

little knowledge.

What was it Sir Isaac Newton said?

'I do not know what I may appear to the world; but to myself I seem to have been only like a boy playing on the seashore, and diverting myself in now and then finding a smoother pebble or a prettier shell than the ordinary, whilst the great ocean of truth lay all undiscovered before me.'

Living as I do near the north coast of Cornwall, I often look out on to the Atlantic. Our lives are governed by the clock and the calendar, but standing on the cliffs at Tintagel you begin to see things in some sort of perspective: a clock's relation to the thing known as Time is less significant than a bath full of sea water to the ocean.

The sea change in supernatural matters is interesting. In 1981 readers of the *Times* were asked in a questionnaire about their beliefs. Significantly, over eighty per cent said they accepted telepathy and ESP, and this figure represented a substantial increase over the proportion in a national poll fifteen years earlier, when more than half said they did not believe in telepathy.

The calibre of the men and women exploring the paranormal is another important fact. They are not like Lewis Carroll's Queen who could believe six impossible things before breakfast. Whether we are investigating astrology or dreams, palmistry or time-slips, it is essential we keep our feet firmly on the ground.

James Turner, who lived at Borley, site of 'the most haunted house in England' told me of an incident there. This lady, 'keenly interested in Borley,' arrived one afternoon, when James was disinfecting his mushroom beds. She sniffed the air and he explained the nature of the smell in the garden 'that it had nothing to do with the supernatural.' Nevertheless next morning a national newspaper carried the headline 'Odd smell at the most haunted house in England.' She had clearly rung the newspaper with news of her supernatural discovery.

I recall too someone writing to me from the United States, enclosing photographs of ghosts in St Nectan's Glen. Alas I could find no ghosts – nor could anybody else here. There were shadows in the glen and on the prints – and yet the photographer was convinced the shadows were, in fact, ghosts.

1995 marks an important personal milestone.

It was on Midsummer Eve 1965 that I had my first encounter with the supernatural. As a result of that experience around midnight new doors – and windows – began to open. Those mysterious lights inside Bossiney Chapel were to have a profound influence. The fact is the supernatural has enriched and become an important facet of my life.

A lesson from these thirty years is that if one seeks one does indeed find, but – and it's a rather crucial but – the search goes on. 'Take life one day at a time' is a good motto; yet one can never 'end' thinking and searching. There is the need to keep eyes and mind open for new evidence – and most limits exist only inside the mind.

At this point I would like to say something about the importance of seeing paranormal matters in perspective. Here the breadth of my interests helps. Publishing and writing during the last twenty years have embraced more than 200 titles and a wide range of subjects. In 1994 I became a writing and publishing consultant, thereby creating a new dimension. Outside and beyond all that, animal

BOSSINEY Chapel on the outskirts of Tintagel. Phantom lights inside these four windows on Midsummer Eve 1965 produced more than a strange experience. That episode on the stroke of midnight, shared by four other people and a terrier called Tex, marked the beginning of my investigations into the paranormal. At the time, I did not know the significance of these lights illogically coming on and equally illogically going out – and thirty years on I am no nearer a solution to the puzzle but I am grateful for the strange event which set me on the road towards the unknown.

welfare and cricket remain worthwhile causes – and Sonia and I continue to be keen theatre goers. All of which gives variety and a sense of perspective.

It is quite wrong to assume all investigators into the paranormal are occultists or members of some esoteric club or organisation. Take the case of Alfred Watkins, who on a June day in 1921 riding his horse across the hills near Bredwardine, perceptively noted that prehistoric remains, together with many religious buildings dating from pre-reformation times, fell into alignments. Fieldwork confirmed his belief and he called these lines 'leys.' In a sentence the concept of the ley system is simple: that *sites of ancient importance align*. Watkins, then in his mid-sixties, was a brewer and Herefordshire magistrate, a keen photographer and amateur archaeologist, a lover of the English landscape and fascinated by ancient locations. His was a sudden vision of old straight tracks criss-crossing the countryside.

Or we can look at an earlier character. Sabine Baring-Gould was more than an expert on Devonshire mysteries and curiosities, he

THE RUINS of Glastonbury Abbey have a strong sense of the past. I ▶ *have had three reports of strange happenings here at Glastonbury. The latest, and appearing in published form for the first time, concerns a certain Jerry Brooks. On a visit to the Abbey he became separated from the rest of his party and found himself by the High Altar. Suddenly Mr Brooks was aware of a ghostly procession proceeding towards it. He could see the features of the priest leading the procession quite clearly, but no one else's. He watched whilst the priest conducted his service from start to finish. Apparently none of them was aware of his presence – that, at least, was the impression they gave. His niece, who lives not far away in Avon, told me: 'I discovered Uncle Jerry was psychic when one day driving in East Anglia, I said I liked the **feel** of Norwich better than Ipswich, to which he said he was on the board of six hospitals, and you could take him blindfolded to any one of them and he'd know which it was. "Good heavens!" I said, "you must be psychic." "I am", he replied, and he proceeded to tell me how he had seen the ghost of a dead fellow officer during the war. After that he was never afraid of ghosts, and interestingly he was a hard-headed man of business...nothing airy-fairy or imaginative about him.'*

wrote of murders discovered by the employment of divining rods in a church. Furthermore the murderers were tracked down by a man using his dowsing rod! Dowsing, of course, has been tradition-ally linked to the thing we call 'second sight.' The Rev Sabine Baring-Gould, who was born in 1834 and died in 1924, was the squire and parson of lovely Lew Trenchard on the edge of Dartmoor. A real all-rounder, he wrote many books on fiction, folk-lore and mythology and is perhaps best known for his hymn *Onward Christian Soldiers*. His old home has a haunted reputation, but he was a man of wide interests and certainly not obsessed by the supernatural.

Nandor Fordor said 'The battle against the unknown is gradually being lost – or rather, won – by the new generation of scientists who are finding themselves more and more in Alice's Wonderland where nothing is impossible.'

The mind remains the most baffling puzzle of all. Science has transformed – and continues to transform – the world in which we live, yet the scientist knows as little about your mind and mine as he ever did.

One bonus in the last three decades has been a greater spirit of tolerance and co-operation. Police, at various times and in different countries, use psychics to help in finding missing people or in their search for solutions to other serious crime.

Dowsers are employed to locate subterranean water. More and more patients are being helped by spiritual healers; 'fringe and alternative medicine' are no longer dirty words.

We have come a long way since Charles Fort, who was born in 1874 and died in 1932, the man who has been called 'the father of modern phenomenalism.' He coined the phrase 'teleportation' and was probably the first person to speculate that mysterious lights in the sky might be craft from outer space. Charles Hoy Fort, who was born in Albany, New York, accepted everything that happened in nature and rejected interpretive myths, including those from sci-entists. His name lives on in the *Fortean Times*, a bi-monthly maga-zine of reviews and research on strange phenomena and experi-ences. Mr Fort's dictum 'One measures a circle beginning any-where' expressed his Continuity philosophy in which everything is in an intermediate state between extremes.

I have long been fascinated by the differing attitudes of church people about our subject. I have corresponded with two bishops and interviewed a third here in our cottage in North Cornwall, all of whom showed a sympathy and understanding of the supernatural, but equally I have met some church members who have implied investigators into the supernatural are suspect characters, possibly even slightly mad.

One Westcountry parson who must have had a respect for the subject after a certain church path experience was the Rev Dr A.T.P. Byles, then vicar of Yealmpton in Devon. It was in the late 1940s, and on this particular evening the vicar went to meet his wife who was 'doing flowers' in the church. As he came up the path Dr Byles saw a hole in the path, something like three feet in width. Mrs Byles, on coming out of the church, also saw the hole. Husband and wife went off to get a plank to cover the dangerous hole – and came back with a Yealmpton builder. They were astonished. There was no hole to be seen. Did they experience a time slip?

Despite multiplying evidence of psychic phenomena, some scientists seem unable – or unwilling – to accept much of the evidence. The scientists, or, at least, the majority live in a world of only repeatable experiment.

It is fair to say the history of ghost photography, particularly during Victorian and Edwardian times, had more than its fair share of charlatans with the camera, producing fakes.

Ray Bishop, the doyen of Cornish photographers, tells me: 'There is less scope for fake photographs today. The automatic camera with the automatic exposure means there are fewer opportunities, though somebody using older equipment could still fake a ghost shot.' Ray has in his possession the photograph of a ghostly figure in a West Cornwall church, taken by the then vicar. 'Is it a real ghost?' Ray had no hesitation: 'I'd say it is a very genuine photograph by a very genuine man.'

Some years ago the celebrated Arthur C Clarke featured in a television series and in one episode he investigated the realm of strange photographs. One photograph revealed a ghost-like image near the altar inside Newby Church, Yorkshire. The photograph, taken in the 1960s, was the work of the Rev Kenneth Lord. Mr

Clarke challenged the Home Office laboratory team, and Dr Steve Gull and his Home Office colleagues could find no certain scientific explanation for the figure. Dr Gull's verdict? 'Of all the pictures I've looked at this is the only one which could be an actual ghost.'

The same series also produced a photograph, taken in 1959, of an Ipswich taxi-driver Jim Chinnery sitting alone in his taxi. The photographer was Mabel Chinnery, wife of the driver. When the photograph was printed, the driver was no longer alone in the car. There sitting in the back was his dead mother-in-law.

In general, inside these pages, I am concentrating on cases in what we call the Westcountry, roughly an area from Bournemouth across to Bristol and all the way down to Land's End at the beginning or the end of Cornwall. Occasionally though, I have gone beyond that defined territory for the purpose of giving a more complete picture of our subject – and subjects.

One such case concerns a ghostly warning in the 1880s. Lord Dufferin, the guest at a country house in Ireland, woke during the night and looked out of the bedroom window. There in the garden he saw a phantom walking across the lawn with a coffin on his back. The noble lord dashed out into the garden and asked the man what he was doing. No reply: the strange figure vanished, but that was only the start of the story. The second instalment came some ten years later when Lord Dufferin, the British Ambassador to France, was attending a reception in Paris. The Ambassador was about to enter the hotel lift when he recognised the face of the lift operator. It was the same face he had seen that night in the Irish

KING JOHN'S Hunting Lodge at Axbridge. This building, now a museum of local history and archaeology, is reputed to have two ghosts: an attractive lady from Elizabethan times dressed in white, and a phantom cat. It was formerly a Tudor merchant's house. Though ghosts do appear in some modern buildings, they seem to favour very old properties. I believe this may all be tied up with very basic mathematics: the older a house the more people have lived there or been connected with it in some way and consequently the greater the chances of a ghost. As for the feline spirit of this old hunting lodge, the animal has been seen by archaeologists on several occasions – and always in the evening.

garden. Lord Dufferin refused to enter. Moments later the lift crashed to the bottom of the shaft, killing all the passengers – and nobody discovered how or why the mechanism had failed.

We shall be looking at more ghosts later.

Over the centuries millions of reports from all parts of the globe have been recorded: experiences which come under the broad umbrella of supernatural. It is difficult – even impossible – to sweep all these happenings under the cynic's carpet. People do cheat and lie. Others may hallucinate but assuming just one experience in a hundred is genuine, then a solid mass of evidence remains.

The painter Jean Cocteau was once asked: 'What do you look for in art?' The Frenchman thought for a few moments and then replied with conviction: 'It must astonish me!'

Come with me to the *Edge of the Unknown*. Now and then you too may be astonished.

* * * * *

ATMOSPHERE, TIME AND DREAMS

A T THIS early stage I would like to examine two important questions. First, what is atmosphere? Secondly, is atmosphere a key factor in the supernatural quest?

Collins English Dictionary gives as many as seven definitions for the word atmosphere. Within a supernatural context, I think we are discussing the prevailing mood, tone or feeling, and probably all three inter-relate, producing that something we call 'atmosphere.'

We talk of people 'creating an atmosphere.' This often means when people are angry or anxious, their anger and anxiety rising above everything else. A business friend discussing a shop which had recently changed hands, remarked 'It no longer had a friendly atmosphere.' I knew precisely what she meant: the warm welcome of the previous owner had gone.

My favourite hotel in this part of Cornwall is the Tredethy Country Hotel at Helland Bridge on the edge of Bodmin Moor. It so happens Sonia and I know the owners, Richard and Beryl Graham, who invariably receive us warmly, but outside and beyond their personal reception, there is a friendly atmosphere about the place.

Many writers build up 'atmosphere' in a supernatural story – and, as a writer, publisher and consultant, I can understand why, but in my experience as an investigator into psychic phenomena, things frequently occur in a very matter-of-fact way.

The truth is some ghosts are solid, conventionally dressed figures, behaving in a thoroughly normal fashion until they suddenly vanish into thin air or walk through a heavy closed door. I recall James Turner, the author of *Ghosts in the South West*, published by

JAMES Turner, the author, in his younger days. When we first met he was living in a house near Wadebridge, reputed to be haunted by three monks. At the time he was working on a book about ghosts in the Westcountry. James had a theory that many ghosts were so lifelike many people went through life never realizing they had seen one.

David & Charles back in 1973, saying he thought a small percentage of people we saw in our lifetime were, in reality, ghosts.

Interestingly, when a ghost appears or phantom footsteps are heard the temperature usually drops but oddly enough one thermometer may drop by several degrees whereas another will show a perfectly normal reading.

On a visit to haunted Dockacre House, Launceston, North Cornwall for a radio series called 'Ghost Hunt,' I was conscious of the third step on the main staircase seeming much colder and somehow different from the rest: no menace, just that very, very cold sensation. There is no doubt investigators regularly find a haunted area to be very cold. I have known a cynical media man come out in goose pimples – even when no ghost had appeared! – and when the Ghost Club Society visited the Bush Inn at Morwenstow in May 1994, two members found themselves in a very cold area of the bar which was, in fact, one of the haunted spots of the old inn.

After years of interviewing and researching, I have come to the definite view that people respond to atmosphere in different ways – the sensitive picking up most, which *may* mean only a certain kind of person sees ghosts. But the cynic, of course, can have a Road to Damascus experience. I once interviewed a retired Army sergeant major, the type of soldier who had put the fear of God into his young recruits. Explaining how his cynicism had been killed – killed for ever – through his encounter with a ghost, he said 'Now I disbelieve *nothing*!'

*HAUNTED Hound Tor on Dartmoor. It is believed Sir Arthur Conan Doyle came here, and some say his novel **The Hound of the Baskervilles** grew from that visit. What did the novelist and spiritualist make of the vibrations? In his book **The New Revelation**, published in the last year of the 1914-18 war, Sir Arthur described how he had initially been cynical about the reality of the paranormal, but he became a convert. During those war years he referred to 'something really tremendous, a breaking down of the walls between two worlds.'*

Dartmoor, of course, is full of atmosphere; menacingly so for many people. Great Hound Tor, south of Manaton, is a location which numerous visitors find uncomfortable, even unbearable. Some have fallen into a trance here. Personally I find it beautiful and energising. Yet sometimes I have felt someone is watching, and when I have looked around I have been a fraction too late to see who or what it was.

More than once on the moor and on Bodmin Moor in Cornwall, I have felt right at the edge of the unknown . . . just one more thing to happen and then *breakthrough*. Maybe out on the moor, on ancient landscape, we are closer to the beginning of things. In the end is our beginning or something like that?

It could be that atmosphere is all tied up with time. The great J B Priestley had some clear-cut theories on the subject of time. He reasoned there are three forms of time: 'ordinary time' when I stand on the station platform waiting for the train; 'inner time' which is when I am quietly contemplating, moments of serenity; and 'creative time' when a writer or painter or sculptor occasionally experiences a phase of 'great intensity.' Mr Priestley reckons he once wrote four complex plays at top speed – in his own words 'like a man watching himself run at headlong pace across a mine-field.'

That very fine literary all-rounder Denys Val Baker once told he often found it difficult to get started at his writing at the beginning of a day, but he was very aware, at times, of feeling inspired. 'I've learnt to recognise that spirit,' he said, 'to respond to it . . . days when the words almost come pouring out, almost as if somebody else were writing them.'

Denys Val Baker had a very strong sense of premonition too.

On one occasion he attended a party at Newlyn. 'I'd had an uneasy, uncomfortable feeling all day.' On the way home his car turned broadside and rolled over twice. He was injured, but, in a way, lucky to tell the story.

Then, on a boat trip to Scilly, he had gone ashore to the New Inn with friends, but again had 'this feeling of unease.' Later that

◀ *I HAVE long held the view that many manifestations are possibly linked to time, but recently I came across an unusual case relating to time in another sense. Mollie Sullivan, in a telephone conversation in January 1995, told me how twice in her life, 'when experiencing an emotional condition, worried or upset, in one case the break-up of a relationship, my wrist watch and clocks in the house, including battery-operated clocks, have stopped. No rational explanation. But after I'd got them working again, they went on perfectly for a year. In some strange way my emotions have simply stopped them. I'd like to know how and why it happened.'*

Next day I consulted Shirley Wallis, astrologer and teacher of creative meditation, and this was her concise, considered reply: 'What occurs is the electro-magnetic field of our physical bodies is overly charged by emotion. It's quite common and I've had it happen many times in my own life.'

evening when the Val Baker party steered their way out of the harbour, somebody asked 'Where's the boat?' Denys told me 'I shall never forget that traumatic moment . . . she's aground. She's on the rocks!'

He also had a curious writing experience when he used the cottage of a friend in West Penwith as the setting for one of his stories. 'I attempted to capture the elemental side of life in Cornwall,' Denys explained. He was very attracted by the hills and moorland, and in this story he coupled the landscape to the Bohemian lifestyle of artists and writers, bringing the tale to a climax with a mock observation of ancient Druidic sacrifices. 'In my story there was a death and I was shaken to find out later that in real life there was a similar case of someone going to spend a night there only to be found dead next morning!' Denys called it 'a sort of pre-vision.'

Anyone interested in this fascinating subject of time should read John William Dunne's book *An Experiment with Time* which was first published as long ago as March 1927. Mr Dunne was no crack-

SONIA Williams, second from the right, entertained members of the Ghost Club Society to a Cornish cream tea on their visit to North Cornwall. On her right is the natural healer Nelson Side of Camelford who answered questions about his work with people and animals.

pot. The son of a General, born in 1875, he was an old school army officer 'crossed with a mathematician and an aeronautical engineer.' He was not a time-haunted man either like J B Priestley, but he was a driven man, trying to discover a personal theory about time, strangely compelled to make some sense of the precognitive quality in his dreamlife. At the very outset of *An Experiment with Time*, he states:. '. . . this is not a book about occultism . . .' That may be so, but I now realise no serious collector of paranormal publications should be without this book.

Anyway here is a combination of events which would have intrigued both J B Priestley and J W Dunne. On Monday afternoon I was working on the start of this chapter. That night I dreamt about time and a clock. On Tuesday morning I was committed to two calls on Dartmoor on business, and, driving across the moor, I decided to call at the Dartmoor Bookshop at Ashburton, on the offchance. 'Please, have you a copy of Dunne's *An Experiment With Time*?' I asked Barbara, the proprietress. She immediately produced a copy of the 1934 edition. I certainly had no intention of searching for a copy when I started this piece of writing on Monday afternoon. So what do we make of that?

* * * * *

MARGO Maeckelberghe, the distinguished Cornish painter at work in her studio at Penzance, agrees with JB Priestley about 'creative time'. 'When things are going well,' she says, 'it's amazing how time goes. You suddenly find three or four hours have gone. Yes, you do have these bursts of great intensity. Some paintings come together in a very few hours. Others seem to take years!'

Although she paints abroad, and has done so in several countries, we Cornish people love her native paintings. Margo Maeckelberghe's work goes beyond the beauties of coastline and moor, sea and sky, she captures the brilliance of the Penwith light and the colours, the atmosphere and often the mystery. Like J.M.W. Turner, she turns rain and storm into vivid memorable art.

'In my experience "creative time" is a period of great and sometimes frenzied intensity,' she reflects. 'Sometimes with results which can amaze the artist, and by artist I mean composer or writer as well as painter or sculptor. There is a feeling of staying outside time, and physical things like cold and tiredness are completely ignored. My studio is large and largely unheated and this rarely affects me when I'm working: many occasions I've worked away for say three hours and not bothered to turn on the heater . . . not noticed the need for heat. Maybe there's an inner heat or something.

'But sometimes there's a reluctance to enter your studio and I've spoken with other painters who experience the same reluctance. Then you say to yourself "I'd better go to the studio" and often that reluctance becomes a fallacy. Once you're in the studio there's a commitment beyond yourself, and in an odd way time has nothing to do with it, time by the clock that is. Yes, Ernest Hemingway may well have had something when he said "good writing comes easiest and best when you're cold and hungry", but I simply don't feel either when I'm into creative time.

'I've just come back from Jordan, and on these journeys you're either putting your clocks forward or back. You're interfering with time and time itself is a vast mysterious subject . . . so many dimensions like things seen through Alice's looking glass.'

MYSTERIES

MOST of us love a mystery – the deeper the better. But we must remember there are mysteries and mysteries. Some come within the definition of *supernatural*. Others do not – yet still baffle us.

Despite the advances of science and technology, mysteries remain. The more we discover, the more there remains to be defined and explained.

What, for instance, are we to make of the Bermuda Triangle?

This part of the Western Atlantic, off the south eastern coastline of the USA, is an expanse of water which has been the setting of bewildering mysteries. Planes have seemingly vanished into thin air, and ships have disappeared without trace – or logical explanation. Hundreds of lives have been lost, yet not one body, nor a single piece of wreckage has been recovered.

Are there forces at work which, at present, we do not recognise or understand?

John Blashford-Snell in his superb book *Mysteries, Encounters with the Unexplained*, published back in 1983, wrote:

'Only a few years ago, it was popular to scoff at the Loch Ness phenomenon, but with the introduction of sophisticated underwater detection equipment, many *bona fide* scientists are saying 'There must be something there.' If we believe that an enigma is a fact that cannot be explained in any usual manner, then perhaps a new approach is needed to unravel it. This does not necessarily call for a person of high intelligence, but quite simply for one with an inquiring mind and determination – someone who is driven by insatiable curiosity. It is curiosity that drives most modern explorers on.'

THE SCORHILL stone circle on Dartmoor. On my one and only visit to this circle, I remembered the painter and writer Charles Simpson who first introduced me to moorland magic. He told me: 'The inscrutability and antiquity of the stones put them beyond the definite . . .' and he spoke of 'the mysterious thrill as you walk inside a ring of stones.' I am a frequent visitor to our Westcountry stones, especially those circles on Bodmin Moor. Some people experience a mild shock from them as if the stones themselves contain some form of battery. That has never been my experience, but I do find they have a healing quality: a balanced sense of relaxation and rejuvenation. I remember hearing Barney Camfield speak about healing and he said something to this effect: 'If we are in a state of relaxation then life energy can flow freely through our bodies.' Well, often that is how I respond to a stone circle.

As a member of the Ghost Club Society, I have been impressed by the sincerity and integrity of fellow members, men and women seeking paranormal experience and explanation. Many of us have long believed *homo sapiens* is endowed with a sixth sense: impulses reaching the brain due neither to hearing nor sight, smell nor taste – extra-sensory perception.

Dennis Wheatley, the man they called 'the master of mysteries,' once reflected: '. . . everyone has this sense to a greater or lesser degree . . . In primitive peoples it appears to be much more highly developed than in advanced races; possibly because the many preoccupations caused by enormously varied social activities overlay our inherent spiritual resources.'

Undoubtedly invisible influences are at work. Could it be that there is some form of radio set inside our human brain? If that is so, and if tuned in to the right wavelength, then this radio set can send out messages and receive them.

Coincidences are often part of some mysterious process. We have all experienced linking events that have seemed too bizarre, too perfect to be the product of sheer chance.

One day I called on a bookshop in Cornwall, where I knew the owner would be settling a bill for more than £500. Unfortunately I had been unable to make an appointment, and, on arrival at the shop, one of his assistants told me 'He won't be back for another four hours.' It was impossible for me to wait that long: an afternoon of calls on other shops in other towns lay ahead. Sitting in my van, I recalled a recent conversation with Barney Camfield who had been advocating the importance of visualization. Quietly, I visualized the book shop proprietor coming back. Then I turned the van and there coming up the road was the man himself. 'The pattern of my day changed suddenly,' he said, 'and I came back . . .'

A minor event perhaps, but one that leads us naturally to these questions. Which comes first: fact or fiction? Does art reflect life? Or can the impossible happen and the reverse occur? These are relevant questions when we think of the opera star Marie Collier who in 1971 was discussing good future plans with her manager when she opened her window and fell to her death. Marie's last role had been Tosca who leaps from a wall – to her death.

On the subject of death, a reader from Devon recently wrote to me about a very odd death on Dartmoor. The body of a man was found in a crevice out on the Moor in 1976. He was attired in a grey suit and shoes that hardly suggested he was exploring Dartmoor on foot. Near the corpse were a bowler hat and an attache case. The man's shaving gear was set out on a ledge. He had no driving licence, no documents of any kind in fact. It were as if a piece of

Agatha Christie fiction had been turned into reality. All the mystery man had on him was a little money, a bottle of laburnum seeds (poisonous) and some capsules of cyanide. Incredibly no poison was found in his body, and forensic science failed to determine the precise cause of death and, despite police investigations, his identity remains unknown.

One of our great Cornish mysteries is the saga of the so-called 'Beast of Bodmin Moor.' I caught a glimpse of him in May 1993, and wrote about it in *Psychic Phenomena of the West*.

A more recent and dramatic encounter in October 1993 concerned a 37-year-old woman who was knocked out by a blow to the head as she walked her dog shortly after midnight on the edge of Bodmin Moor. When she came round, the woman said she was face to face with this puma-like animal. She told the police the animal had its head lowered and its rump raised in a classic big cat

◀ *THERE is no doubt equines do feature strongly on the paranormal scene in the Westcountry. There have been numerous ghostly sightings of horses, ponies and donkeys. Recently I was told an interesting riding account – no equine ghost this time. Avril Greenaway was riding her pony, and her mother was very preoccupied alongside her, riding a lively racehorse. It was 7.30am and they were at Launcells Barton, near the site of an old monastery, when Avril, looking over the hedge, exclaimed 'Look!' There's a woman coming up the field.'*

Avril recalls 'she was faceless, wearing a yellow top and reddish-brown long skirt, and carrying a whip.' Her mother could see nothing – just an empty field – but Avril had no doubt whatsoever. So vivid was the woman that she later did a drawing of the figure, for her aunt Diana Dennis who told me: The woman she saw clearly belonged to an earlier time, and probably had something to do with the old monastery.'

There's nothing ghostly about our photograph here: Tracey Collis riding one of her horses near Camelford in North Cornwall. Tracey, who breaks and trains horses locally, says: 'Horses are very sensitive in their own way. They do sense things. An animal has been killed by the roadside, it doesn't have to be there, but they have a sixth sense and pick up the presence of the dead animal though it's no longer there. And if you're out riding and feeling upset over something, the horse will often pick up your emotions. They have this ability to sense and sum up people.'

stance. The moon was out, and the animal only thirty feet from her. She scrambled the short distance to her residence near Cardinham as her labrador growled and barked at the strange animal.

A doctor later confirmed she had injuries consistent with a blow to the back of the head. In a field close by a local farmer found a sheep had been savaged. Only a few days earlier a decapitated sheep had been found in the vicinity after it had been dragged across a field and over a wire fence. A veterinary surgeon said the animal's injuries were not caused by a dog, fox or badger, but by a large carnivore.

Joan Amos, who lives at Peter Tavy on the edge of Dartmoor, has a theory about these animals. Mrs Amos has thick files concerning UFO sightings all over the world, and has been a co-ordinator of reports and groups since 1978 – and believes there could be a link. 'There have been so many cases in which animals have been seen on board these space ships,' she told me. 'There was the case of Allen Godfrey, the Todmorden policeman who was abducted. On his return he was regressed and spoke of seeing a black animal on board; he said he could not tell if it was a cat or dog.'

Missing people come into the category of mysteries.

On an August afternoon in 1978 a girl called Genette Tate, then aged thirteen, vanished in Devon – consequently launching a massive investigation. Yet Genette has not been seen since that warm summery afternoon – not a particle of evidence as to how or why she disappeared.

These are the last known facts of her young life. On the Saturday afternoon of August 19, Genette cycled from her home village of Aylesbeare to collect newspapers from her usual pick-up place on the Sidmouth to Exeter road. She did a newspaper round with the evening papers and by 3pm she was cycling back towards Aylesbeare. In Within Lane she passed two school friends Tracey and Margaret. These two girls caught up with her when Genette dismounted to push her cycle up a short but fairly steep hill. Genette then got back on to her bicycle, rounded a bend and went out of sight – seemingly out of life. She had travelled only 300 yards before *something* happened. When Tracey and Margaret came round the bend no more than five minutes later, they saw

32

Genette's cycle lying on its side, its back wheel still spinning. Some papers had fallen out of the saddlebag. There were no signs of a struggle, and neither girl had heard anything unusual.

Seventeen years on, Genette Tate's disappearance remains a tragic baffling puzzle.

Certainly fact is sometimes stranger than fiction. Here is a true but haunting train experience.

In October 1928 two young children were killed in a railway accident at Charfield, Gloucestershire, when the Leeds to Bristol express crashed into a goods train and burst into flames.

There were sixteen casualties, and fourteen were identified. The two unidentified victims were the children, a boy aged about twelve and a girl thought to be half his age, both badly burned. The ticket collector, who survived the crash, remembered seeing two children board the train alone at Gloucester. He said they were wearing school hats. Part of a breast pocket of a school blazer was found with a school motto, Luce Magistra, as well as two new nine-inch-long shoes and part of a sock with the initials CSSS.

Yet tailors and shoemakers over a large area were canvassed without result. Schools, churches, advertisements yielded not a single clue.

Surely someone was waiting for them at the first and only stop? No result there. No relative, friend, teacher, neighbour reported or knew of them.

Eventually the children were buried, the railway authorities taking the responsibility. More than sixty years on, the identities of those children remain a brace of mysteries.

Here in the Westcountry we had a decidedly eerie train which became known as the 'ghost train.' The 1.20pm which ran from Newton Abbot to Paddington acquired quite a reputation. Train driver Mr J Hibber, who lived not far from the station at Newton Abbot, was taken ill on it. At Exeter station they took the sick man to the waiting room and he died within a matter of minutes. Only a few months earlier Fireman Powerlessland departed this life as the same steam train came into Paddington station, and in November 1927 Fireman Walters was killed, getting the engine ready for its London run: three deaths within a space of less than twelve months.

Down in the south west, some of our biggest mysteries are probably the stone circles.

William Crossing, the author of that Westcountry classic *Crossing's Guide to Dartmoor*, published in 1912, ventured various possibilities for their existence and purpose: 'that they were intended for gymnastic performances; that they were part of serpent temples; that they formed the professional roads of the Druids; that they were race courses; that they were once roofed and formed shelters; that they represented armies drawn up in battle array; that they were intended to guide people over the moors in misty weather; that they have an astronomical significance; and that they are a representation of passages that led to the chamber in a tumulus...'

Eighty years on, we are no nearer the answer. In fact, more possibilities have been added to the jigsaw puzzle. Guy Underwood thought the circles – or the majority of them – stood over blind water springs. Did the priests of the ancient religions know this? The generative force of nature? These circles produce more questions than answers.

Tom Lethbridge believed they were charged with energy, which visitors from outer space could have homed in on, and Colin Wilson has told me a 'power emanates from these stones.'

This much I know: a visit to a stone circle for me is invariably a worthwhile experience, a recharging of the batteries. One comes away from them with a heightened sense of well-being – as in the case of spiritual healing. It is a fact that when Rudyard Kipling, a man who had spent many years in the East, made his very first visit to Batemans, his seventeenth-century house in Sussex, his response was positive: 'We entered and found her spirit, her *feng shui*, to be good.'

The same at the stone circles? I think so.

THE HOLY GRAIL

KING Arthur's magic and magnetism lie in the fact he changes his shape to suit the needs of each new age. Arthur is the embodiment of a dream, an ideal.

More specifically Arthur is all about a search – your search and mine – and at the very heart of it all is the effort to find our best self.

In pursuing the Grail Tradition we are indeed at the Edge of the Unknown, like light glimpsed at the end of a dark mysterious tunnel.

The original meaning of the word 'Grail' was not 'Holy' in the usual Christian sense. Long before the birth of Christ, the concept of the Grail existed. *Collins English Dictionary* defines Holy Grail as 'Noun in Medieval Legend, the bowl used by Jesus at the Last Supper. It was brought to Britain by Joseph of Arimathea, where it became the quest of many knights...' Of those knights only the spiritual Percival was successful.

The Grail, like many other pagan ideas, was absorbed by the Christian Church. It became a symbol of ideal, of purity and quality, particularly after it had become an important section of the Arthurian cycle of legends.

These beautiful stories, these legends of chivalry, are really veiled accounts of man's eternal search for truth, and here in the Westcountry we have strong Arthurian associations in Cornwall, Somerset and Dorset.

Shirley Wallis, who lives at Plymstock on the fringe of Plymouth, has been studying Arthur and allied subjects for some years. She is an exponent of psycho-expansion, an astrologer, tarot card reader, healer and teaches creative meditation. In fact, she is able to encompass many other metaphysical subjects.

I asked her how she saw the Holy Grail, and this was her reply.

'I also see the Grail as a complex and beautiful symbol. But what does this symbol represent? What does it mean? Since every person is unique, so the meaning and understanding to them will be unique, based upon the quality of their desire to *know*.

'In the film 'Excalibur' released in the early 1980s, the character Merlin spoke of there being many Merlins, many Arthurs, many Knights of many Round Tables – and all are come again, to remember and to bring forth Truth. He went on to say that only the Grail can redeem and restore, (through its qualities). Merlin qualified this by telling Arthur that because he, Arthur, loved him, he was able to return, a dream to some, a nightmare to others! I found this idea most interesting, since prior to the film's release I had been engaged on research involving the ability to move into what we call the past and future, observing 'other times', one of which was around 500AD, the Arthurian period of the Dark Ages and Merlin's words resonate with what I discovered. My desire to know more of the underlying mysteries has increased and developed over the years.

'I understand the Grail to represent both a vessel and a quest, not only for each individual – although this is where it starts and remains – but for a country which is moulded by its people. I also understand the Grail to be of particular significance to the United Kingdom as we make the transition from the Piscean Age into the Age of Aquarius. Isn't it interesting that the symbol for the astrological sign of Aquarius is that of a human holding a vessel and pouring water? I see that vessel as the Grail. The water I see as knowledge through Love and Light. I am told that Love is creation and Light is information: to become enlightened about something. When this occurs we carry that frequency within ourselves and thus develop as a Grail vessel in human form: becoming 'informed'.

'From the Grail, the creative force of love intermingling with the light of information becomes more and more refined as we accept and allow it to flow without the human conditions with which we so often label it. Then we have the wisdom and comprehension of

what unconditional love really means and our own Grail vessel can radiate its unique frequency of harmony.

'So, I see the Grail as my quest – my training programme to absorb and discover the knowledge that is offered, gradually building a Grail vessel within my human form to be expressed through my own understanding of love and light.

'When Merlin said in the film Excalibur, "a dream to some – a nightmare to others", I think it all depends on your point of view – your way of seeing, your method of questing – of asking the right questions – the quality of your desire to know. The difference between the illusion of doubts and fears and negative thinking (the nightmare), and the enlightenment through vision, creativity and positive thinking, (the dream), is free will. The choice to become and also serve the Grail *is ours*.'

◀ *THE ARTHURIAN theme has fired some fine art. Here is an example: Arthur as a babe being handed to Merlin from the postern gate at Tintagel in North Cornwall. This oil painting, by the Victorian artist W H Hatherell RI, can be seen at King Arthur's Great Halls, Tintagel. It is part of an impressive array of Arthurian pictures, oils, painted in the figurative style and all based on descriptions in Malory's* **Morte d'Arthur**.

THE DIVERSITY
OF GHOSTS

I HAVE spent thirty years investigating the supernatural – thirty fascinating, rewarding calendars. Interviews and researches have led me into different facets of the supernatural but my greatest interest lies in ghosts, and the nature of ghosts.

Back in 1993 I wrote *Supernatural Investigation*, and in it devoted a chapter to the theme 'What is a Ghost?' I put this precise question to five different people whose opinions I greatly respect: Colin Wilson, Peter Underwood, Barney Camfield, Lori Reid and Jack Benney. That single chapter aroused enormous reaction and comment from readers and reviewers. I do not propose to resurrect the question or their answers here; instead I want to examine another area of the subject: the range and the variety of ghosts.

Most of the time the dead lie quiet in their graves or the ashes of the cremated have scattered and disappeared, but now and then strange things happen – as if those dead people are revisiting us in our world of the living.

Death has been called 'the final frontier' and yet . . .

Ghosts come in different forms. A phantom can appear as real and solid as you and me. It can be transparent and insubstantial. There can be wisps of smoke, strange smells – some fragrant, others unpleasant – sounds, defying human explanation, and atmospheres which range from the peaceful to the spooky.

There is a theory nothing is ever totally lost. Our words, our deeds, even our thoughts are somehow preserved for ever – and occasionally something of that past returns, visible or audible, to the here and now.

In researching stories of ancient ghosts, one occasionally comes across an amusing element. A certain property had a genuinely haunted reputation, and an exuberant boy placed a trussed hen on top of the four-poster in the spare room. When the guest turned in for the night he heard persistent scratching above and believing it to be some troubled spirit from 'the other side' ran into the corridor wearing little more than his night cap!

There was the case of a lady staying in a house alone, the family being away, and she experienced an uncomfortable sensation in the bathroom, irresistibly drawn to the window; so much so that in the end she shut it tight. She later learnt a former owner had suffered from deep depression and had thrown herself out of the bathroom window.

In some cases we learn the identity of the ghost. Mr Charlton Shaw spent a disturbed night at the Naval & Military Club in London. Waking up in the early hours of the morning, he observed a woman beside his wife's bed. He asked if she was all right, but she did not reply. Putting on his bedside light, he discovered his wife was fast asleep – and the other figure gone. Later he learned the ghost of Lady Caroline Lamb, Byron's lover, haunted the club. Caroline Lamb died after hitting her head on a mantelpiece.

Now and then one can speculate as to *why* a ghost haunts a certain place. The famous suspension bridge at Bristol was the work of Isambard Kingdom Brunel who died in 1859, five years before the bridge he designed was opened; and it is his ghost walking in the shadow of his great achievement. Reliable witnesses have given detailed descriptions of the phantom: a figure in double waistcoat, high-collared cut-away overcoat, breeches and top hat – and smoking a cigar. Brunel was only fifty-three when he died: a combination of overwork and too many large cigars.

An eerie psychic legacy of the last war is an airman who has been observed parachuting from the sky at East Cowes on the Isle of Wight. I wonder what tale lies behind this airborne manifestation.

Another interesting case concerns Eugenie, who when she worked as lady's maid to a large family, stayed in a certain house temporarily. She was allocated a bedroom with a small dressing room leading off it. One morning as it was getting light Eugenie saw a girl in white emerge from the dressing room. The girl walked to the mirror, looked at herself, then turned and walked to the foot

LOOKED at herself, then turned . . .

A STONE Age warrior riding a shaggy horse . . .

of Eugenie's bed and stood there. She then appeared to 'fall backwards.' Eugenie lay in fright until a maid brought her a morning cup of tea. 'Quick! There's a girl under my bed!' There was nobody under the bed. Later, when she told her experience to the resident housekeeper, Eugenie was shown a picture. 'Was this whom you saw?' The girl in the picture had died of TB, and her family would not go near her for fear of catching the disease.

In all my researches I have come across only one instance of a ghost appearing to order – in response to a challenge in fact. I was interviewing Betty Lukey, then well-known in North Cornwall for her clairvoyant powers, and asked her: 'Have you ever seen a ghost?'

'My father, Frederick Rowley Lake, was a director of James Hawker, the wine merchants of Plymouth,' Betty replied. 'He was a disbeliever. So I said to him "In view of your disbelief I'll come and haunt you if I go first, I'll come and blow you a kiss! But if you go first you must come and see me . . . and let me see and smell that old Harris tweed jacket you should have thrown away years ago." It was a year after his death, and I was then living at Crantock and I came across him sleeping in a deckchair. He was wearing his old Harris tweed jacket, his glasses had fallen on his lap and his panama hat had slipped forward . . . just as he'd been when he'd been with me at Crantock two years before.'

Here in the Westcountry we have probably the most ancient ghost recorded in the world: a Stone Age warrior riding a shaggy horse, galloping across Cranborne Chase in Dorset. The man, wearing fur skins, rides the animal without bridle or stirrups. They have been seen in the region of the Roman road to Old Sarum. They have also been observed near the prehistoric site on the Chase.

Dorset has another historic phantom: a Roman soldier with sword and shield, helmet and toga. He has been seen standing some two feet *above the ground*. When approached, the Roman vanished into the evening air. The interesting thing about this particular case is that it was observed by no less than fourteen people and the Roman ghost was standing on the level of the road when first constructed in the first century – and not the 1969 level of the road, the year of the sighting. Little wonder then that we feel a strong

*SOMERSET has a strong supernatural quality. One person who under-stands that fact is Rosemary Clinch. She is the author of **Supernatural in Somerset** and co-author of **King Arthur in Somerset**, and lectures in Metaphysics at Yeovil College.*

sense of the past in certain places: the supernatural influences of long dead Romans, Normans, Cavaliers and Roundheads.

Haunted properties have a long history.

Andrew Lang, who studied the subject deeply, had this to say: 'haunted houses have been familiar to man ever since he has owned a roof to cover his head.' Sightings have been reported inside the primitive huts of tribesmen and castles, crofters' cottages and monasteries. Saint Augustine wrote about hauntings as 'familiar occurrences' but apparitions of living men and women are relatively rare.

There is no doubt ghosts are a problem for the scientist. Peter Underwood in his book *Ghosts & How to see Them*, published by Anaya in 1993, reflected: 'There seems to be a striking paradox in psychical research, for science today, by its own laws, is being forced towards what would, up to now, have been regarded as an unscientific attitude. Every scientist worthy of the name has to admit that the world is a far more complicated place than it was once thought to be, and almost daily the scientific world edges towards accepting psychical research as a science.'

I hope and believe the 21st century will produce a new frontier: an area where the paranormal will meet science. Moreover I have a hunch at this new frontier the nature of ghosts will be explained and maybe that will tell us about the afterlife.

It is an interesting fact that monks feature in a good percentage of ghostly sightings. Their spiritual characters or their devotion to a particular place? Maybe something of both.

I am indebted to my friend Claire Wolferstan, who lives at Worle, for the following two accounts: 'Claire (no relation) went downstairs to fetch her book, but as she approached the stairs to go up again she was astonished to see the figure of a monk ascending them. She watched his sandalled feet ascending step by step and followed him. However, halfway up was a small landing and on reaching this she was horrified to see the feet turn and begin to descend the stairs towards her. As she pressed herself against the wall behind her, she felt icy cold air come past her on the landing.'

The second incident concerned a property in Oxfordshire.

'A friend named Rosalie was house-hunting with her father, and as they descended the staircase, after viewing the upstairs of a property she saw a monk coming up the stairs and in fact passing them. Later on she enquired of her father "Is that a religious foundation we've just seen over?" He replied not that he knew of and why did she ask. "Oh I just wondered because of that monk we met on the stairs." Her father exclaimed, "Monk! What monk? *I* didn't see any monk." Later they learnt that the place had had some connections with a monastery!'

Time-slips can and do occur.

Here is a case relating to a place not many miles from where I am writing these lines.

Patricia Treleaven, who lives at St Tudy, told me: 'The path goes up to the moors, and on the left there is an old house, too large for a cottage, too small for a farm, with lovely barns and outbuildings, long uninhabited. It is still used by horsemen.

'The first time I went up there, I was alone, and I was delighted to see this pretty old place, with a nice garden, and a little girl playing outside the garden wall, with an old-fashioned doll's pram, like the one I had as a small girl, over seventy years ago. She had long dark curls, and a "Railway Children" pinafore, in blue, with flared frills over the shoulders. I smiled at her, and she smiled back shyly, and then I thought I might seem intrusive staring at the house, so I walked back down the lane among the flowers and trees, and the ancient stones covered in moss which might have been the remains of long-gone settlements. I rejoined my friend and the two dogs playing in the ford – the water is crystal-clear and I think there may be otters, though my search for spraint has so far yielded nothing. I never said anything about the child and the cottage, just took the whole thing for granted, until some weeks later we met two people on the clapper bridge, who got into conversation with us, and remarked that they came on holiday each year, and would like to buy the old house – "But," they said, "The owner won't sell and of course, it is so dilapidated, and the garden all gone to ruin, it would need a lot of money spent on it . . .' I was just about to open my mouth to say: "But it's NOT dilapidated, and there are people living there." Then I thought – No! Things like this have happened to you before – keep quiet.

'The only way was to revisit the place – and sure enough, it WAS somewhat in need of redecoration and repair. The garden WAS in ruin, though I found the well easily, hidden in the waist-high grass and weeds. I contacted a friend who is trained in these things, and asked her to come with me – I did not say anything about my experience, not wishing to "muddy the water". She immediately picked up my small girl, plus other children, and a man sitting outside the barn, busy shoeing a horse.

'My feeling is that I fell through a hole in time, and saw the place as it was at the turn of the century.'

As a member of the International League for the Protection of Horses and the RSPCA I have a particular involvement in animal welfare, and as a member of the Ghost Club Society I have a natural interest in animal cases.

Not long ago I came across a fascinating publication entitled *Animals in the Spirit World* by Harold Sharp, published by the Spiritualist Association of Great Britain back in 1966. Harold Sharp, a highly rated medium recalled:

'Courtney Thorpe, a well known actor in Victorian days, kept and loved a number of small dogs. He lived to be a great age, and although he had no fear of dying, was always very distressed as to what would happen to his dogs. He had arranged that a small legacy should be paid to a friend on condition that this friend "adopted" his canine family. Some years after his death an elderly woman came for a sitting. I saw clairvoyantly an old man surrounded by excited dogs jumping around him, and sometimes jumping around her. During the years one by one they had left the home of their adoption to bound forward through the invisible door to their original owner and friend who awaited them in the spiritual realm. Now he was sending most grateful messages to his old housekeeper. I was told that while the dogs were still on the earth he almost haunted the woman's house where they were housed; but since they have gone to him in the spirit world, his presence is rarely felt.'

There is no doubt animals do feature strongly in paranormal accounts. Alan Nance, the Cornish spiritualist and healer, told me some mediums, in his experience, insisted on having their pet dog or cat present during a seance, believing the animals 'give power.'

Cats, of course, are the most common animals in psychic phenomena, and the tradition of ghostly felines goes back a long way –

A BLACK cat is reputed to bring us good luck. He is a familiar image of mystery, associated with magic and religion – appropriately this character is photographed in a Somerset chuchyard. In more general terms the cat is said to represent the intuitive and the instinctive qualities. Cats often feature in our dream life. Here much depends on the dreamer's attitude to cats and how the cats behave in the dream experience. Cats were domesticated by the Chinese, some 5,000 years ago, the Egyptians worshipped their cats and rated the killing of a cat as a more serious crime than manslaughter. Cats have long featured in the traditions of the sea. Sailors considered a cat on board ship as a good omen. When a ship came to grief, the cat was invariably one of the first to be saved. The old folk, too, saw the cat as a kind of weather forecaster, believing that if the cat washed behind its ears, then it was going to rain.

to the Ancient Egyptians in fact when cats were worshipped as gods, and phantom dogs have been reported in hundreds of cases scattered all over the United Kingdom. That celebrated Irish ghost hunter Elliott O'Donnell once said: 'When I investigate a haunted house, I generally take a dog with me, because experience has taught me that a dog seldom fails to give notice in some way or another – either by whining, or growling, or crouching shivering at one's feet, or springing on one's lap and trying to bury its head in one's coat – of the proximity of a ghost.'

Certainly in my first major supernatural experience at Bossiney on Midsummer Eve 1965 the behaviour of our terrier Tex was confirmation that something very strange was taking place – for a few minutes around midnight he underwent a personality change, courage suddenly deserting him. His reactions, as much as the four people present and may be more so, underlined the fact we had seen lights switched on and off by no human hands, defying all logical explanation: ghostly lights no less.

My brother-in-law Owen Edwards, who lives just across the border in Devon, has a boisterous liver and white springer spaniel by the name of Buster, an animal who lives up to his name. Owen told me: 'In the evenings, especially during the winter months, he'll often sit bolt upright and stare at the door as if someone or something is about to enter the room. Then he'll follow this invisible something across the room to the corner where my television set stands. That corner of the room was once the door leading to the next door cottage. I'm told monks built and occupied this property when they were building the original church.

'Interestingly, when the vicar came to the cottage for the first time he said "The spirits here are friendly." I've never seen any ghosts, but Buster certainly sees something, sometimes two or three evenings in the same week. This something will wake him up from a deep sleep, but it doesn't disturb him because after a few minutes he'll curl up and go back to sleep . . . all very strange.'

Many of us believe horses, as well as dogs, have an ability to sense the presence of ghostly character. There have been instances of horses neighing repeatedly outside a property where someone is dying. There have been cases where horses have declined to enter a haunted area. I know of one Cornish wood in which horses

behave oddly and some become terrified on the approach to that wood.

We recognise the fact horses can show an extraordinary degree of sensitivity. What are we to make of the events on the 17th day of June 1951 at Spinadesco near Cremona at the funeral of an aged Achille Alquanti? The dead man had lead a deeply religious life, but his sons, who were atheists, insisted on a civilian funeral. Their father would not have approved of such a decision. Anyway the horses, drawing the funeral carriage, were passing the local church when they knelt down and refused to get up for some considerable time. Did the dead man inside the coffin somehow transmit to the horses his desire for a religious ceremony?

I have long held the view that manifestations of dead people and dead animals indicate there is some form of life after the thing we call death for both people and animals; but honesty compels me to admit one serious reservation. Here I refer to ghostly *objects*. There has been the haunted chair at Rossal House, Sunbury-on-Thames; there have been haunted chests. Here in the Westcountry we have the case of the Iron Chest of Durley in Somerset: its mysterious opening and closing is reputed to have prophesied the death of John Bourne. In North Cornwall in the heart of Parson Hawker's Country, I have heard stories of a poltergeist chest at Stanbury Manor.

Surely not phantom chairs and chests in the after life?

Ghostly vehicles add another dimension. In February 1994 Mina Lethbridge, widow of Tom Lethbridge, eminent explorer, archaeologist and investigator of the occult, told me 'I was driving Tom to Exeter on a misty afternoon. We were on a rather narrow road near Honiton. I saw a rather ancient square-looking saloon car approach-

◀ *BUSTER, a lively springer spaniel, who seemingly sees things invisible and unknown to his owner Owen Edwards. One of my earliest investigations was into a ghost dog seen near Tintagel. There is no doubt phantom dogs do appear in the Westcountry. Devon, in particular, has had a number of black dog sightings.*

ing and drove slightly into a grass verge to make room. Just as it reached us it appeared to turn sharply to its left into a gateway and vanished! I do remember that the grass at the roadside seemed long and lush more like early summer grass – it was November. I turned to Tom and said "Did you see that car do that?" He had seen nothing. We went back next day to see if a car had gone through the gate, but obviously nothing had been through it for a long time. The car appeared to be stone coloured.'

Yes, great diversity.

* * * * *

GRAPHOLOGY

GRAPHOLOGY is a systematic method of endeavouring to read character from the handwriting of a person. As a collector of autographs for more than forty years I have a keen interest in the subject. It is interesting to see how a young sportsman's signature, written say in the 1950s measures against the same autograph signed today.

Sometimes the change is quite dramatic. The age gap is even more dramatic in the case of a handwritten letter. One exception to this rule is the great Australian cricketer Sir Donald Bradman. I first obtained his signature forty years ago, and I recently wrote to Sir Donald asking if he would kindly sign a card for framing alongside an action photograph. The two autographs were virtually the same.

Dame Daphne du Maurier generously autographed many of her books for me: the first in about 1960 and the last shortly before her death in 1989. Her signature too retained the same flourish and character all through those years.

As a cricketing connoisseur, many of my autographs are cricketers. An especially interesting signature is that of Walter Hammond, the majestic England and Gloucestershire batsman; I have, in fact, three autographs of Wally Hammond: the first as a young cricketer, the other two later in his career when he made the big social leap from 'player' to 'gentleman' and had become England captain. The later autographs have greater flourish, style and confidence.

At a lunch one day I had the luck to sit next to an experienced detective who explained how an expert in graphology had been a

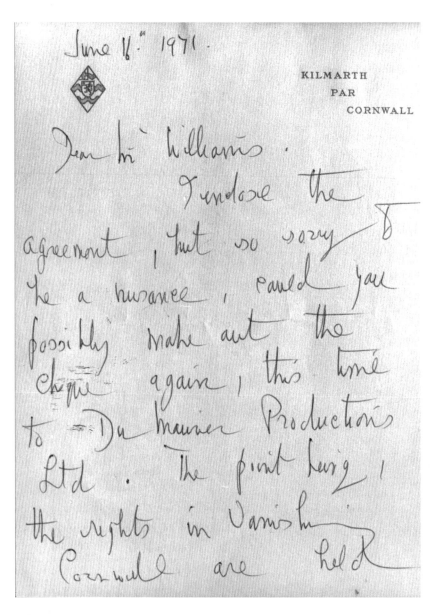

June 16." 1971.

KILMARTH
PAR
CORNWALL

Dear Mr Williams.

I enclose the agreement, but so sorry to be a nuisance, could you possibly make out the cheque again, this time to Du Maurier Productions Ltd. The point being, the rights in Vanishing Cornwall are held

STYLE and flourish, character and charisma in this sample of author Daphne Du Maurier's handwriting.

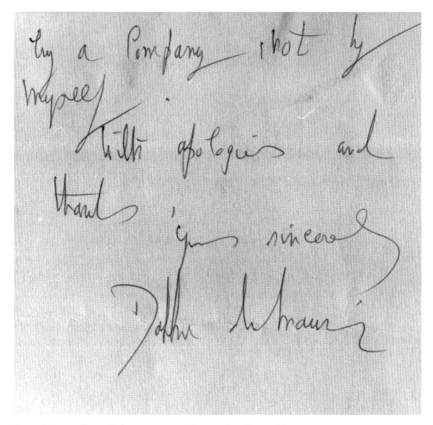

key figure in solving a complicated crime. Even doodles on a telephone pad had been interpreted, and helped to put together the jigsaw pieces.

As a writing and publishing consultant I see manuscripts from widely differing people. The punctuation alone can tell us a great deal about the author. Dots and dashes rather than commas and full stops are generally the signs of the enthusiast.

Too many exclamation marks not only lose their effect, they usually signal the author has plenty of imagination but that he is in danger of exaggerating.

Full stops have telltale signs too. The person who leaves out a full stop is probably a lazy writer; whereas the big black full stop is the sign of the lover of life's pleasures.

If the writer's handwriting slopes down from left to right, he or she is pessimistic. If, in contrast, the handwriting goes upwards from left to right, the writer is optimistic – at the time pen was put to paper anyway. Perhaps we are being told 'things are looking up!'

Large writing invariably comes from men and women who are proud, people possessing high ambitions or ideals, and often both. Such writing also reflects self-confidence and a sense of importance.

Very small writing, on the other hand, can mean either a love of detail or a small and sometimes petty mind, an inclination to pay too much attention to trifles.

Capital letters tell us a good deal too. Well-formed capitals convey energy and will-power.

The barring of the Ts, our margins, the endings of words: the subject is a vast one, worthy of an entire volume.

After so many years as an autograph collector, I am quite convinced writing is not simply a guide to character, it is a first-class guide. The person who signs hurriedly, another who writes when tired: the signs are inevitably there.

I have alongside, as I write, the autograph of Sir Gordon Richards, who was champion jockey 26 times and rode an incredible number of 4,870 winners on the race course: the skill and the style are there in his: 'Best Wishes, Gordon Richards,' the underscoring of his signature reflecting that great horseman's courage. As Sigmund Freud put it: 'There is no doubt that men also express their character through their handwriting.'

It has to be admitted some writing does contain contradictory traits. But is that all that surprising? Are not many of us a mixture of contradictions?

GHOST STORIES
– and OTHER BOOKS

FICTIONAL ghost stories have long been an important part of the publishing scene. The number of ghost stories, collections by either an individual or a team of writers, runs into thousands.

Montague Rhodes James is probably the master of the British ghost story, a character who spent the greater part of his working life occupying senior posts at Eton and Cambridge University. His books have become collector's items. Another eminent figure in this field was Algernon Blackwood who will be remembered as 'the ghost man' by many radio listeners and television viewers. A mystic writer of the highest order, Algernon Blackwood had that special talent of building up uncanny atmospheres out of seemingly ordinary situations which is, in fact, the enigmatic quality in many real supernatural cases. In addition to his novels, Mr Blackwood wrote a rich harvest of short stories. His *Tales of the Uncanny and Supernatural*, first published more than three decades ago, shows his mastery of the mysterious and the macabre.

A third man who wrote novels with an occult background was Dennis Wheatley. He served in the 1914-18 war as an officer in the Royal Field Artillery, and in the second world war he was a Wing Commander on Sir Winston Churchill's Joint Planning Staff of the War Cabinet.

The author of over forty bestsellers, Mr Wheatley considered reincarnation the only logical explanation for an afterlife. He had tremendous energy as a writer: in one brilliant burst he produced a book containing 170,000 words in just seven weeks.

Charles Dickens wrote arguably the most celebrated ghost story of them all: *A Christmas Carol*, published way back in 1843. The popularity of that book encouraged Mr Dickens to write a ghost story each Christmas.

It is not a well-known fact that Dickens came to North Cornwall, and there is an interesting story about haunted St Nectan's Glen near Tintagel. Here his friend Daniel Maclise RA painted a delightful portrait of a shoeless girl with a pitcher on her shoulder and a dog in the foreground. The novelist was very keen to acquire this painting; so much so he bought it under an assumed name. The girl whose dress 'is simply but tastefully arranged, falling in graceful folds and enclosing the beautiful symmetry and proportion of the figure' is believed to be Georgina Hogarth, the author's sister-in-law.

Outside fiction, a real industry of supernatural titles has developed, and I am fortunate in having Midnight Books just across the Tamar in Devon. Steven and Frances Shipp operate their business from The Mount, Ascerton Road, Sidmouth; their prompt and friendly service has ensured the steady growth of the supernatural side of my library.

'I started Midnight Books in early 1989,' Steven recalls. 'It grew from interests in the unexplained, folklore, legends and so on, and love for secondhand books. I have always delighted in ferreting around secondhand bookshops . . . these places are very special with their rows of dusty books and the smell of musty paper. The name comes from my little black cat Midnight. I had been trying

▶

COLIN Wilson, one of the greatest writers on the paranormal in the history of the subject. His **The Occult** *is rated one of the most thought-provoking books in the twentieth century. Cyril Connolly, reviewing it in the* **Sunday Times**, *had this to say: 'I am very impressed by this book . . . by its erudition . . . by the marshalling of it, and above all by the good-humoured, unaffected narrative charm of the author, whose reasoning is never far-fetched . . .' Colin Wilson who lives with his wife Joy on the south coast of Cornwall believes that we human beings possess not simply one 'self' but 'a whole hierarchy of selves'. One of my favourite books is his* **Afterlife**. *In it he assesses the evidence from voices-in-head experiences of psychiatric patients to clairvoyants and psychical research.*

for a name to call the business when in strolled Midnight. It seemed the perfect name to conjure up the atmosphere for the kind of books I sell.

'Midnight Books has grown from strength to strength since then. I married Frances in October 1991, and she now helps out with book buying, computer work and numerous cups of coffee. Our little daughter Griselda, who was born in March 1993, also helps with rearranging the books. We issue four mail order catalogues every year – January, April, July and October – each one carries over 450 titles covering a wide range of books on the unexplained. We also have a free book search service.

'My interest in the unusual has woven its way into the pictures I paint in oils. They are very detailed landscapes of Devon into which wander strange and mysterious figures, personifications of nature, the seasons, green men . . . I have had several one artist exhibitions and my work has been shown on BBC South West television.'

One of my favourite authors is Colin Wilson who lives down on the south Cornish coast. His titles include *The Occult, Mysteries, Poltergeist!, Access to Inner Worlds, The Psychic Detectives* and *Afterlife*, and he is co-editor of *The Directory of Possibilities*.

Another is Peter Underwood, who was President and chief investigator of the Ghost Club for over thirty years, and has probably heard more first-hand ghost stories than any man alive. Peter is Life President of the recently formed Ghost Club Society and generally acknowledged as Britain's number one ghost hunter. He is a

◀ *PETER Underwood, Life President of the Ghost Club Society, signs a copy of his book* **Haunted London** *for Michael Williams on the Society's visit to Cornwall in May 1994. Mr Underwood, who has written forty books on the paranormal and allied subjects, has conducted world-wide tests in telepathy and extra-sensory perception. He is a long-standing member of the society for Psychical Research and in 1987 was elected a Fellow of the Royal Society of Arts. His published works include* **Jack the Ripper, One Hundred Years of Mystery** *and* **Death in Hollywood** *in which he charts the sometimes strange or macabre last hours and days of famous characters who lived and died in Hollywood.*

valued contributor to the Bossiney list – and his recent titles include *Nights in Haunted Houses*, published by Headline, a collection of night-time investigations. In his own words: 'I investigate phenomena as scientifically and dispassionately as possible.'

Both these writers, personal friends, have been valued contributors to the Bossiney list. Authors whom I never met but rate highly, include Tom Lethbridge and Brian Inglis. All Tom Lethbridge's books deserve a place in the library of every serious student of the subject. He once reflected: 'What is magic today will be science tomorrow,' and those eight words somehow sum up the style and spirit of all his books – and the man himself. As for Brian Inglis, his *The Paranormal, an Encyclopedia of Psychic Phenomena* is a classic of its own kind.

Anyone wanting an introduction to the paranormal would do well to acquire *The Illustrated Guide of the Supernatural*, a beautifully illustrated book originally published by Marshall Cavendish in 1986 with a Foreword by Richard Cavendish. It is a thoughtfully compiled volume – specialist contributors writing about *their* aspects of the wide subject: alchemy and alien animals right through the alphabet to white magic and the zodiac.

Collectively and individually, books on the paranormal do various things. Many of them satisfy a desire to be entertained – and possibly be frightened – by the supernatural. Many readers want books that tell of events which cannot be explained away.

Maybe Lewis Mumford got close to the heart of the matter when he said: 'The ultimate gift of conscious life is the sense of the mystery that encompasses it.'

Last but certainly not least a salute to Lyall Watson for *Supernature, the Natural History of the Supernatural*, originally published in 1973. Cosmic law and order, man and the cosmos, the physics of life, mind over matter, signs of the mind, transcendence, the cosmic mind and new dimensions, it is a fascinating survey and remains a tour de force. The perceptive Cyril Connolly, reviewing it in the *Sunday Times*, said: 'Dr Watson is concerned with the correspondence between human life and this "vast organism", and between the organism and the cosmos . . . *Supernature* is one of the most open-minded books to come my way,' and *Books and Bookmen* referred to it as a 'resounding bomb of a book.'

SOME favourite books by some favourite authors from my supernatural library.

One of the most important books on the supernatural in the last quarter of a century, it deserves a prominent place in any worthwhile library on our subject.

*   *   *   *   *

AIR DISASTER

I am indebted to Jean Slough, who lives at Roborough, Plymouth, for this incredible story. It happened in August 1966. Here is Mrs Slough's account – in her own words.

I HAD flown from Luton International Airport taking with me my sister's child Leslie as a treat. I was also accompanied by my husband who, like me, was on a week's holiday. It took fifty minutes to reach Blackpool and as we had left early in the morning we had a long glorious day in the sun. We returned to Luton at about 8.30 in the evening. Just as we crossed the tarmac I stopped to admire a gleaming silver Britannia airliner. It was being loaded by baggage handlers. Our flight had been on a much smaller aircraft. I stopped to admire the shining magnificent plane saying: 'I'd give anything to be travelling on that.' My husband hurried me on, Leslie's parents waited, he said.

Later, fast asleep in bed my husband woke enquiring in a tone of extreme anxiety. 'What's that noise?' I sat up. Fire bells rang. There were cries, urgent screaming calls. We dived out of bed. Something disastrous had obviously happened at the airport. We lived as the crow flies about two minutes from it. Houses and buildings hadn't sprung up all around like it is today. We had a clear view of the airport. There was an awful lot going on, all unseen activity. We stood at the open window, the moist chilling air coming in at us, trying to make out what had happened. There was nothing, nothing to see, it was all sound, terrifying sound. Frozen, demented, we returned to our bed.

I rang my sister Kathy whose boy Leslie had travelled with us on our lovely day out. I told her there had been an air crash. I knew it was a terribly late hour to ring someone but I felt I'd got to tell someone, especially as Leslie had been entrusted to me on the trip earlier and I mentioned how lucky we were, it could so easily have been our plane. I told her to listen to the early morning news on the radio at six and she would learn all about it (we didn't have news bulletins in the sixties during the night). She would, she said shakily.

On the stroke of six I switched on, there was nothing out of the ordinary. Usual Middle East crises. The country wasn't into rapes and drugs yet. No old ladies being mugged for their pensions and certainly no fatal air crashes. There was no mention of planes.

What was it all about? I felt so utterly sick and foolish. Whatever did my sister and her husband think of me ringing in that distressed voice at that ungodly hour? I tuned into every news bulletin. There was nothing serious, not a mention of an accident. Did we hear it? Did it happen? Had we gone round the twist? The answer came at around eleven o'clock that morning. We took a bus into town. The bus pulled in to the stop beside the newsagents stand. There it was emblazoned on the news-stand in startling scarlet ink, scaring the living daylights out of us.

'Britannia air crash – 138 killed' (the biggest air crash ever for Britain). The total fatalities were not as high as they had printed but it was still the most dreadful crash ever.

We bought a newspaper. Whilst my husband ordered stiff drinks at the nearest pub I read about the heart-rending air disaster. My husband took in my white anxious face. 'It didn't happen here,' I gasped. 'It was in Yugoslavia.' I was ready to drop. 'What?' was all he said, taking the newspaper from me and staring ahead in solemn concentration. 'What's it all about?' I croaked, parched lipped. 'God knows,' he said, struggling gallantly not to show the flickering fear in his eyes.

The reason the authorities kept it from the press for as long as they did was there were many, many flights that dreadful night. They didn't want stampeding passengers; flying was a relatively new experience for most those days. There were relatives to inform of the terrible disaster. A limited number of air officials knew of the accident. There was no way we could have known.

I was terribly relieved to hear from three articulate people who had a similar experience. A reporter was at the airport investigating stories of sightings of flying saucers. (I held a responsible position at the airport.) I told him of our totally unexplainable traumatic experience when we had 'heard' the plane crash. It was printed in the local paper. I received three letters from people in the area who

IT IS *an interesting paranormal fact that some ghosts only manifest them-*
selves in certain weather conditions. I have reports of ghostly sights and sounds
in stormy weather. Did some disaster occur in a storm? And does wild weath-
er somehow trigger their re-appearance? I am inclined to think just that. The
nature and the unlocking and unleashing of ghosts remain some of our greatest
mysteries.

too had experienced almost the same. They had 'seen'. Theirs was visual. Appallingly realistic. A vision of the plane's destruction. One man wrote he was in bed and in his mind's eye was desperately fleeing from the carnage, sweating, demented, escaping the fury of gigantic flames, flaming trees and fuel-spattered wreckage. He awoke fighting for breath, panting and huddled in a heap, drenched in sweat. His wife thought he was having a heart attack. He described the painfully vivid scene to his wife exactly as it appeared in print later, a distinguished man, a Doctor of Medicine, he asked me specifically not to disclose his address.

Two others had an almost identical blindingly blazing experience. They too, wished to remain anonymous mentioning how frustrating the whole reeling scene was, mutually agreeing with me and my views describing it as a terror-soaked nightmare.

* * * * *

COLOUR

THE INFLUENCE of colour – and colours – on the minds of men and women has stretched across the centuries.

We can go back to the vivid colours of the temples in Greece and Egypt, travel – physically or in the mind – to Tibet and India where colour has long been an important part of meditation.

Colour therapy is based on the theory that colours affect people to such an extent some colours can help improve the quality of health and happiness – and serenity. Coloured lights have been successfully employed in the treatment of patients with mental disorder. Peter Underwood in his scholarly *Dictionary of the Supernatural* said: '. . . occultists believe that since disease is a vibratory disorder, and colour therapy affects the vibrations, a diseaseless future will eventually be possible for mankind.'

Mr Underwood, who is the Life President of the Ghost Club Society, goes on to say: 'The colours of the spectrum are usually considered to rise from the lowest, red, through orange, yellow, green, blue and indigo to the highest, violet, and the qualities of the respective colours have been detailed as follows. Red: strength and wrath, mastery; orange: pride, life force associated with the physical state; yellow: prudence, intelligence; green: temperance, the link between nature and the supernatural (the middle of the spectrum); blue: justice, perfection; indigo: love, spiritual mind and intellect joined to the soul; violet: hope, the working of inner forces.'

It was Rudolf Steiner who renewed interest in the therapeutic value of colour in a series of lectures in the early 1920s. Consequently colour therapy has become an established part of alternative medicine.

SIR WINSTON and Lady Churchill visiting bomb-battered Plymouth during the war. An accomplished painter in off-duty hours, Winston Churchill said when he reached heaven he intended to spend the next million years painting. But one person who doubts that is psychic Scorpio subject Claire Wolferstan who says: 'He'll want to return to earth long before that, for his soul's evolution and possibly for some specific mission.' In his lifetime Sir Winston frequently responded to hunches and intuition and his son Randolph claimed he once saw his dead father sitting in the leather chair at Chartwell. There was nothing quiet about this encounter between father and son because they engaged in a lengthy and detailed conversation about people and events – and the transformation in world affairs over the previous fifty years.

Responsible research has revealed that different colours make different impacts on our nervous systems. Colours are put into two temperature categories: warm colours, like orange, red and yellow, are seen as aggressive, advancing shades whereas cool colours, such as blue, green and violet, are regarded as receding and passive. In tests in the laboratory, for example, red actually stimulates the nervous system, pushing up the blood pressure and quickening the heart rate – but blue does precisely the opposite.

Some believe that in studying colour we are, in fact, looking at a force of great power – that we are opening ourselves up to the world of healers and healing.

On the supernatural scene grey is often the dominant colour, the majority of ghosts appearing as grey figures. The phantom cyclist I met on the Camelford-Bodmin road was grey: both the man and his machine.

But reliable witnesses have reported ghosts seen in vivid colour, and some dream analysts believe many people dream in colour, but the shade fades rapidly from memory. Ania Teilhard in her *Le Symbolisme du Reve*, published in 1948, thought coloured dreams are proof of animation in the unconscious and reflect the vitality of the dreamer.

People who know their colours and the influence of colour, rate blue as suitable for women and men of power in all walks of life. It is also considered an ideal colour for the bedroom or a rest room for staff. Red is another strong colour. They say 'a touch of red is good for everyone.'

Our auras too have colour. Psychics say we all have auras, the colour which surrounds the person or animal. Fay Glossop, a Cornish psychic, once told me: 'It's rather like a rainbow . . . but it's not a constant, consistent light. The shades vary according to the moods of the person.' Fay went on to explain that in her healing work the auras were helpful in diagnosis. 'You can tell the very ill patient by the aura. A dull red usually tells me that the person is suffering from some form of cancer. Green and blue I usually associate with nervous disorders.' There is, in fact, a dictionary of colour definitions. Turquoise blue, for example, symbolises high speed thinking and healing work is related to this colour. Orange is the shade of vitality. Chocolate brown stands for orderliness. These are just a few examples.

Dark hair is regarded as lucky, particularly for 'First Footers' those first visitors to a house at the beginning of a new year. But there has always been an odd prejudice against red hair. This could date back to Biblical times for it believed Christ's great betrayer

Judas Iscariot had red hair. Though there is another theory, suggesting this prejudice comes from distant folk memory: the red-haired pirates from Denmark who infested our British coastline.

As a superstitious Celt I am interested in the relationships between colour and luck. I once knew a lady who backed only horses whose jockeys wore her favourite colours, and believe me she did as well – if not better – than many serious punters who spent hours studying form, forecasts, breeding, the going, the course and all the other highly technical matters relating to horse racing.

The Romanies believe a grey horse is a good omen, and I must confess I feel happier and more confident when encountering a grey horse – which may mean luck is largely related to our *feelings* – the person who feels lucky is likely to be more confident, and much of success in life stems from confidence.

Will there be colour in the after life?

One man who hoped so was Sir Winston Churchill. He once declared that when he reached Heaven he intended to spend a considerable part of his next million years painting: '. . . and so get to the bottom of the subject.'

* * * * *

CORNISH HAUNTING

I THOUGHT I knew about all the ghosts and phantoms in this area of North Cornwall, but in researching *Edge of the Unknown* I came across a new haunted property – new to me, anyway.

The former rectory at Altarnun is today Penhallow Manor, a delightful country house hotel. This elegant Georgian style house, built in 1842, stands alongside the village church, dedicated to St Nonna, and known as the Cathedral of the Moor.

Tamsin Thomas of BBC Radio Cornwall and I did a radio interview here: part of our six episode series entitled 'Daphne du Maurier Country.' Dame Daphne was a visitor to the house and her meeting with a former vicar triggered the inspiration for her great Cornish novel *Jamaica Inn*. In the eye of her vivid imagination she made the rectory the home of Francis Davey, the vicar of Altarnun, a key character with his white hair and prominent thin nose 'like the curved beak of a bird.' No more enigmatic personality lives inside the pages of any of her novels.

There have been various ghostly sightings hereabouts. The lady who has been seen walking from the church to the old rectory is believed to be Mrs Tripp, the housekeeper of a one-time vicar. Harry Cleverley, a medium who lives at Merlin Cottage in the village, told me he was consulted by a previous owner of Penhallow. 'Footsteps had been heard upstairs, and I clearly saw this Victorian parson in frock coat pacing up and down in room four, probably working on his Sunday sermon. It's thought two bedrooms are haunted. I'm inclined to think the two bedrooms were at one time just one big bedroom.

'Then one evening in the summer, around midnight . . . the

*PENHALLOW Manor: this lovely old building not only has a haunted repu-
tation, it features in one of Cornwall's best-known novels. Daphne du
Maurier used it as a key location in* **Jamaica Inn**. *Chapters XVI and XVII
are set in the living room of the vicarage as Mary Yelland sat and watched the
smouldering turf fire – and discovered the truth behind her uncle's smuggling.
Dame Daphne told me how she came to Altarnun for the first time as a young
woman on horseback. She stayed overnight in a temperance house at
Bolventor . . .*

street lights were still on . . . I took my dog for a walk in the village
when I saw this entity coming down, almost gliding down the
churchyard path. The dog stopped and raised its hackles and I
went very cold. There is no doubt it wasn't a real person because it
walked straight through the churchyard gate, which was shut. I
formed the impression it was female in a grey gown of some kind
with a hood. This figure walked over the road bridge and disappeared in the vicinity of the post office. They say a woman
drowned at Altarnun in Penpont Water.'

ONE OF the haunted bedrooms at Penhallow Manor, formerly the Rectory at Altarnun. Beyond the window is the majestic parish church, dedicated to St Non – or Nonna – whose altar was probably preserved here. It is hard for us in the 1990s to appreciate that many of the saints had portable stone altars which they took with them. It is an interesting fact that often ghosts are seen in bedrooms – logical perhaps when you consider that many people die in their bedrooms; certainly in olden times. Anyway, there is nothing frightening in this delightful room. The atmosphere throughout this Grade 2 listed building is peaceful. I have stood in the bedroom and absorbed the serenity. The idea of ghosts appearing only in strange places and menacing atmospheres is a fallacy. In our years at Bossiney we regularly heard ghostly footsteps in the quiet cottage alongside the hotel. In addition to the footsteps there were the sounds of a door opening and closing and yet the door itself remained open or closed. It were as if we were picking up background sounds from a tape recorder.

Someone else with memories of the old rectory is Ann-Marie Coles, whose parents ran the country house hotel for a while; she told me: 'There was something slightly unusual about two of the bedrooms. Each morning we'd check each bedroom to see that everything was all right, and often you'd come across these impressions on the made beds, as if somebody had been sitting on them and yet nobody was in occupation at the time . . . very odd really.'

Her mother Marie Gray recalled 'The bedroom overlooking the church was always very cold, and Anne-Marie is quite correct about the strange impressions on the beds. We also had an unusual happening down in the cellar when the knob of the CO_2 cylinder was turned off – and it would have needed someone with strength to do that – and yet nobody was down in the cellar. And our predecessor was absolutely certain she had seen this ghostly lady in grey outside the conservatory.'

Ray Bishop, our principal Bossiney photographer, and I came to the old rectory on a showery morning in October 1994. I had been inside the house only once before, back in the late 1960s when it was still a vicarage. It had a quiet expectant air, rather like Dockacre House at Launceston, there was a good atmosphere about the place.

More than a quarter of a century on, its purpose and name now all changed, the building had retained its serenity. Then it struck me as ideal for meditation, reading and thinking. Now it struck me as the perfect rendezvous for a peaceful holiday, a recharging of the batteries on the edge of the moor.

* * * * *

TEA CUPS
– AND THE FUTURE

IS TEACUP reading merely a matter of old wives' tales? I think not. But then I had a very early introduction to the subject in that my grandmother engaged in a little tea leaf reading for family and friends – and fun.

In fact, as a boy of about twelve I started endeavouring to read the leaves and went on doing it, like my grandmother, on a strictly non-professional basis until about fifteen years ago when I became interested in psychometry and found it a better method of reflecting character and future trends.

Fortune telling from tea leaves is an old craft, probably dating back to as long as tea has been drunk in Britain, but it is a dying craft. The style of tea drinkers has changed so radically: finer leaves to accelerate the brewing time, a strainer so that no leaves gather in the teacup and, of course, most significant of all, the old leaf tea has been largely replaced by tea bags.

I suspect, too, most people wanting a serious reading of their future would prefer to go to a clairvoyant or palmist, astrologer or tarot card reader.

Nevertheless I believe people have been able to *see* for others through the fall and the pattern of tea leaves in the cup. The old-fashioned formula was for the subject to swirl the dregs around three times, usually with the left hand, and then turn the cup upside down before the reader started his or her analysis of the leaves.

There was a tea leaf vocabulary for those who went by the text book. Leaves, for instance, resembling the shape of an anchor were said to indicate a voyage, and a road, represented by two lines of

THE CURIOSITY of men and women to know the future goes back a long way. Maybe people cling to that old theory 'Forewarned is forearmed.' Or perhaps there is greater insecurity than most of us like to admit. Do these tea leaves in these teacups tell us something?

leaves, indicated change, if the lines were straight all would be well, if the lines were wavy there might be difficulties en route.

A bell shape of leaves was reputed to foretell marriage and the form of a key forecast a new home. But as in the case of most – if not all – forms of the prediction business, it was not a matter of knowing and interpreting the symbolic leaves. The truly clairvoyant reader used the patterns of the leaves to focus and sharpen his or her psychic powers.

MANIFESTATIONS
in and around
CHURCHES

SOMEBODY has said 'The supernatural is the natural not yet understood.'

That strikes me as highly logical, and as the Christian faith is all about living and dying, it is not surprising churches and church-yards have been the settings of so many and varied manifestations.

Somerset, which has a high percentage of female phantoms, is fertile ghost hunting country. The grey robed figure, who has been seen inside St Mary Virgin Church at Yatton, is believed to be Lady Isobel Newton. She died in 1498. At St Nicholas Church, Brockley Combe, there have been reports of 'a little lady in brown': a seemingly useful ghost because she has been observed cleaning in the vestry.

Here in North Cornwall we have a church with a murderous past. At Poundstock in 1357 the parish priest William Penvoun (Penfound) was murdered by 'certain emissaries of Satan' on his way from the altar, and two former vicars have told me of parish-ioners who had seen the ghostly victim. One witness thought the life-like priest kneeling before the altar must be the current vicar and soon after was amazed to see the living Poundstock cleric com-ing down the path to the church!

Not far away at Morwenstow people claim to have felt the pres-ence of the great Robert Stephen Hawker, squire and parson of the parish for more than forty years. I interviewed one woman who heard his footsteps coming up the lane from Morwenstow Church; her dog was petrified as the footsteps passed them and continued on their invisible evening journey. She was told 'Mr Hawker often walks this way after a service.'

But sometimes in the past, tales of Cornish ghosts were used as strategy.

The church at Talland down on the south Cornish coast has been the scene of some strange events. The vicar here in early Georgian times was a gentleman named Richard Doidge. It was said: 'Mr Doidge had such command over the spirit world that he could raise and lay ghosts at his will, and by a nod of his head banish them to the Red Sea. His parishioners looked up to him with great awe, and were afraid of meeting him at midnight, as he was sure then, whip in hand, to be pursuing and driving away the demons, that in all kinds of shapes were to be seen hovering around him. Amongst his other eccentricities he was fond of frequenting his churchyard at the dead of night!'

Often, though, the vicar was not alone, for he had a good working relationship with the Polperro smugglers, and, as a result, he embroidered the haunted reputation – so much so that the smugglers found it a very suitable place for storing their contraband. Those 'in the know' were sceptical about Richard Doidge's powers of exorcism. They believed he used the stories of ghosts haunting Bridles Lane, leading from Talland Beach, as a method of scaring off the excisemen. From places like Talland smuggled goods were shifted inland.

◀ *ROBERT Stephen Hawker of Morwenstow, a drawing by Felicity Young of Tintagel based on a sketch by the Earl of Carlisle in 1863. Throughout his life Parson Hawker was very preoccupied with the mystical and the supernatural. He claimed genuine supernatural experience to the extent of seeing Saint Morwenna and, over the years, he became convinced in the power of the Evil Eye, once attributing the loss of nine suckling pigs to a witch's curse. On wild winter nights he would have curious intuitions about those who might need some extra food or bed covering. Prompted by such inner feelings, he would gather together blankets, food and even wine and, accompanied by a servant, would set out and subsequently knock at the door of the cottage in question. Not suprising, then, that the great man wrote a book entitled Ghosts. Morwenstow surely is such a place to trigger ideas along those paranormal lines. He loved all animals – and the birds fluttered around him to be fed. Today he would be in the vanguard of the animal welfare movement.*

However, in general, we Cornish have treated ghosts very seriously. Ghosts frequented the town of St Ives in such numbers that a professional ghost layer was employed well into the nineteenth century.

A curious case of genuine haunting concerned a one-time Bishop of Exeter. For some reason Henry Philpotts chose to live at Torquay rather than Exeter. He ultimately built a villa next door to what is today the Palace Hotel. In due course that villa became part of the South Devon Hotel, and sources say those sections of the building used by Dr Philpotts in his early lifetime have been haunted by a figure in ecclesiastical attire. Witnesses have included both hotel staff and guests.

Bristol Library has rather special memories for me. I often used it during my National Service days at Horfield Barracks in the early 1950s, discovering the beautiful writing of Sir Neville Cardus on cricket and music and J B Priestley on a whole range of subjects. I never had the luck to see the ghostly grey monk who comes to the library to read various books on theology. This monk does not travel far because in his robes he haunts the Cathedral next door.

Time-slips, in the form of religious groups, are fairly rare and always interesting. One such happening took place during Evensong at the church of Combe Martin in North Devon. A member of the congregation, attending that service, saw a door in the screen open and a Bishop – identified by his mitre and crosier – with priests in vestments and a group of laity, both sexes, came into clear view. This ghostly gathering must have been performing some rather special ceremony because men were carrying a model town on a tray.

Combe Martin also had a phantom fiddler. He has been sometimes heard and sometimes seen – and occasionally heard and seen at the same time. A local theory is he is a country fiddler, the kind who faded from the rural scene in the nineteenth century.

'Are there any prophetic ghosts in the Westcountry?' a reader asked recently in a letter.

The answer is 'Yes' and when I last visited the lovely city of Salisbury I thought of the ghostly white birds which fly around the cathedral spire there. Some say it's only a legend but the Doubting Thomases are wrong.

ST IVES in 1910. One of the most haunted towns in the whole of the Westcountry, St Ives employed a ghost layer well into the 1800s.

In 1885 Miss Moberley, daughter of the then Bishop of Salisbury, saw them wheeling above her. Soon after her father died. Then in 1911 Miss Edith Oliver saw the same winged ghosts, and on getting home she heard of the sudden, totally unexpected death of Bishop Wordsworth. How did these two ladies know they were not real white birds? They could see the dark spire through the transparent bodies of the birds.

For one of the most famous religious ghosts of all Britain, we have to go to Westminster Abbey, London. Father Benedictus, a monk, was murdered there in the fourteenth century, but he returns to the Abbey from time to time, often between five and six o'clock in the evening. No vague misty figure, there have been detailed descriptions of him: a tall man, slim, prominent forehead, deep-set eyes and something of a hook to his nose. One witness claimed to have observed Father Benedictus for more than a quarter of an hour, and occasionally he has spoken to visitors before disappearing through a stone wall.

Coming back to the Westcountry I have heard two first-hand accounts of ghostly music coming from empty churches. One in North Cornwall, the other near Tavistock, and written reports of phantom organ music in south Devon.

I was reminded of the link between religion and the paranormal back in 1989 when I asked James Mildren to write *Saints of the South West*. James, writing in the *Western Morning News* on the new publication had this to say:

'. . . when Michael Williams asked me to write a small book on the saints of Devon and Cornwall, I couldn't resist a heaven-sent opportunity to indulge. Michael is often gently lectured about the number of books which he publishes about the "Occult" – and there are a number of Bossiney titles on that topic, but it means, quite simply, the mysterious or mystical, and not the commonplace, sinister meaning which has become attached to the word in the 20th century.

'A book about saints would seem to even up the balance, one might suppose. But to my great surprise, as I was soon to discover, few subjects could be more accurately described as "occult" than a study of the saints of the Westcountry.'

SALISBURY Cathedral seen from the Cathedral School as depicted on an old picture postcard. The spire of this beautiful old building has an eerie reputation. Certainly on visits to the Cathedral I have felt a strong sense of the past, deeper and more spiritual than in many religious buildings.

APPORTING

IT WAS the splendid son of Scilly, Alan Nance, spiritualist and healer, who first introduced me to the word 'apport'.

We were talking at his home in St Austell, and he told me:

'The spirit world's capable of tremendous leg-pulls . . . apporting, that's the capacity of spirit to transport material objects without material aids – I had many experiences of this. Once I lost my bunch of keys. I was so convinced that they'd gone that I had my lock changed and then they re-appeared. No, it wasn't a coincidence or a question of mislaying them. It was one of many instances where things have been apported.'

Only a few weeks ago my friend Claire Wolferstan wrote to me about a strange happening which I intended to use inside the pages of this title. I lost her account – one quite small page but a valuable page within the context of this book. I went through the appropriate file not once but twice: no sign of the missing page. It was obvious Claire's notes had been thrown out with the used envelope; so I wrote a note of apology and asked if she would mind rewriting the account. She agreed.

But here is the curious thing: on the morning I received her second account I found the original here on my desk. Sheer carelessness? I think not. More than once Sonia has said: 'A supernatural somebody must be playing tricks . . .'

Here is a recent letter from a lady, named Kay Marshall whom I met when researching an earlier Bossiney title:

'You may remember me as one of the women you met when you came to see Jack Benney of Bolingey to tell you of our experiences at the lost church.

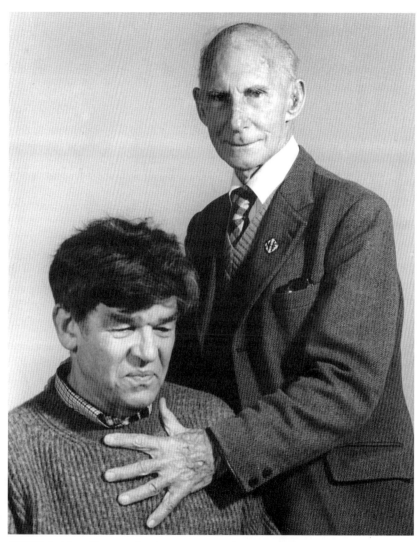

IT WAS Alan Nance who first told me about the curious psychic business of **apporting.** *Here is healer Alan at work on a patient. Initially, I was sceptical on the subject of objects disappearing and reappearing but Alan, a man of absolute integrity, told me how a bunch of keys seemingly vanished into thin air and then came back. He was convinced someone in the spirit world was having a kind of game – and he claimed several other experiences.*

'As we were all leaving the house I asked you what you thought of things which unaccountably aren't there where they ought to be, where you know you put them, only to turn up again right there as if they'd been there all the time. You had an answer and a name for the phenomena. Now I'd like to ask you what it was so that I can put a name to the most blatant bit of that kind of skulduggery I've ever encountered.

'I had a virus and was taking pills every six hours. I had managed to wake up around the right time in the night to take the two pills I had placed conveniently to hand on my bedside table. I could just see them in the half light of 5.30 – 6 am. The last dose was a night one and so I thought as I turned out the lamp 'thank goodness, I'll be finished with those when I wake up,' I duly woke up and could not see them. I put on the light and they simply weren't there!

'I managed to go back to sleep by telling myself I must have taken them absent mindedly, but I didn't really believe it. In the morning they were still not there, not on the floor or anywhere. So I tried not to think about it until dressing to go out about an hour later I turned to look at the clock on the bedside table and, to my horror, there the pills sat – just where I put them! Someone said maybe I just didn't see them before. Yet how could I see them from across the room after missing them twice?

'I would be pleased to hear from you so that I could tell any doubters for my sanity that all this has a name.'

* * * * *

REFLECTIONS
at the EDGE OF the
UNKNOWN

'WHAT do you hope to achieve at the end of your journey to the Edge of the Unknown?' someone asked.

It was a good question and, after some serious reflection, I came up with the answer. 'I hope some people will have removed the blinkers of conventional thinking for a while and I hope others may be encouraged to venture into the *Unknown*'.

In 1973 Lyall Watson, an author with an immaculate scientific background, wrote a memorable sentence consisting of just four words: 'Supernature knows no bounds.'

The last years of this century have seen significant changes in national borders, the breaking down of divisions, freer access from country to country. Many working in the paranormal field believe a similar transformation will take place in our territories in the twenty-first century. In that event the edges of the unknown will change, and that acreage between the real and what is unreal will shrink.

Paranormal or normal? That may well be a recurring question as the future unfolds.

As a cricketer I know the importance of the clearly defined boundary line. As an investigator into the psychic field I believe the edges of the unknown may gradually disappear – and maybe not gradually – because the sheer piling-up of evidence that certain happenings are not what they seem could cause a terrific explosion.

In the last fifty years the distinction between the natural and the supernatural has become less and less. The next fifty years could see that distinction become meaningless.

If we travelled back three centuries we should have met wise men who thought they knew what weight was. But then came Newton who showed that things weigh less on the summit of a mountain – that weight is affected by gravity.

Time has been called 'a rhythm' and that is probably a very correct description, but the passage of time has proved learned men to be liars or fools.

'No man will walk on the moon.' 'No athlete will run a mile in four minutes.' Have we forgotten those confident negative predictions – and a great many more?

Let us, for example, take astrology. I have seen the photograph of a Dutch painting from the seventeenth century: an astrologer in his gloomy study surrounded by the trappings of his craft, a picture of mystery. Whereas astrologers today – those I have met, anyway – prefer to shed this ancient cloak of mystery, making astrology more acceptable, more accessible to ordinary people.

Fat files containing detailed sightings of UFOs, precise reports of people, suffering from all sorts of health problems, claiming relief and sometimes complete cure through healing hands – I have studied the former in a cottage on the edge of Dartmoor and the latter in a house near Brunel's famous bridge which spans the River Tamar.

In a broader sense we have seen 'alternative medicine' become an accepted part of the medical scene, and at a personal level I have seen a natural healer remove inflammation from human and animal patients – like a man turning off the water tap. In Tintagel

BRITAIN has always been a landscape of trees, and five thousand years ago huge forests covered the greater part of these islands. The oaks are the most remarkable of all. All our sailing ships were once built of oak and the giants of ancient forests are preserved in the timbers and panelling of Elizabethan houses and the carved roofs of old churches. Our Westcountry woods are 'peopled' by a number of ghosts. It was George Meredith who challenged us with the words: 'Enter these enchanted woods, You who dare.' I remember meeting the author and poet Ronald Duncan shortly after the publication of his brilliant but controversial autobiography **How to make Enemies**, *and he told me he found woods awe-inspiring places.*

90

Sonia and I knew a Cornish charmer who was so successful in curing warts that local doctors had no hesitation in recommending him, and his success with ringworm in cattle was such that veterinary surgeons recommended him to farmers.

Moreover neither healer accepted – or accepts – a penny.

The intelligent woman or man keeps open eyes, open ears and open mind. When I first interviewed 'King Arthur' two things happened. My views on the reality of the Once and Future King and the whole subject of reincarnation were seriously questioned.

In 1993 I discussed karmic astrology with a pioneer in that field, Judy Hall, who lives in Dorset. She told how she had met people who said they were Boadicea, Gandhi, Lord Palmerston and Tutankhamen amongst others.

Personally I am not one hundred per cent sure about reincarnation. But listen to these words: 'Of course you don't die, nobody dies, death doesn't exist, you only reach a new level of conscious-

ELEGANT Bath boasts a wide range of paranormal activity. Here is Pultney Street. Times were when Admiral Howe, First Lord of the Admiralty, had a residence here. Commander of the Channel Fleet in the French War which triumphed in 'the glorious first of June' off Ushant in 1794, he has been seen on a number of occasions. No vague phantom, Admiral Howe has been observed in very solid human form and wearing his naval uniform. It is an interesting fact that various well-known people of the past have reappeared in the Westcountry as ghosts. Sir Francis Drake, Lawrence of Arabia and King Arthur are just three of them. Is Arthur's manifestation confirmation that he belonged to fact not fiction?

ness, a new unknown world. Just as you don't know where you came from, so you don't know where you're going. But there is something there, before and after, I firmly believe . . .' That was Henry Miller talking in an interview in 1961.

Throughout a lifetime one hears a lot of speeches and orations of various types. Not many are memorable. However on Saturday afternoon July 13 1985 at the City Hall, Truro, I had the luck to hear a brilliant talk by Colin Wilson, seemingly operating without a single note. It was then for the first time that I learned about 'PE' – Peak Experience, a phrase Colin explained as 'times of near mystical joy and affirmation.' The man, who invented the term 'PE', Abraham Maslow believed psychologically healthy men and women have peak experiences fairly often.

In *The Directory of Possibilities*, originally published by Webb and Bower, in 1981, Colin Wilson has written of Abraham Maslow:

'He explained that, as a psychologist, he got bored with studying sick people and decided to study the healthy instead. He quickly noted that his 'alphas', or self-actualizers, were prone to sudden experiences of bubbling happiness – although he was careful to emphasize that these should not be regarded as in any way mystical. He felt that they are a part of the 'human norm'. Moreover, when he discussed PEs with his students, they not only began recalling PEs they had experienced in the past but not really noticed at the time, they also began having more PEs. That is to say, the PE is a function of normal health and sense of purpose.

People might be compared to cars whose batteries run down if they are left unused but charge up the moment they experience a sense of enthusiasm and purpose.'

Exploring the Edges of the Unknown these past thirty years has given me some peak experiences. The diversity has been extraordinary: interviews and correspondence with bishops and astrologers, exorcists and charlatans, ghost hunters and exponents of psycho-expansion.

I have visited castles and cottages, modern council houses and ancient ruins; have watched and listened in a haunted garden in the middle of the night and seen the sun rise from the summit of Rough Tor on Bodmin Moor; have sat at Hitler's desk and received healing in a room full of peace and relaxed energy.

I write these words on a November afternoon as sunlight threatens to break through a moving grey sky. There is an air of expectation hovering over this green Cornish valley.

What a thrilling moment it will be when the truth about ghosts is revealed. What a point in our history when time itself is defined. There are many such prospects ahead. The reality of Arthur? Now *there* is a great expectation, and I believe regression may well produce the answer – or answers. And what about life after death? Thirty years of investigation into ghosts convince me there is some form of survival beyond the grave or the crematorium. Will the Lost Land of Lyonesse reappear beyond Land's End? I have been told this will happen.

These are only some of the exciting possibilities, and I hope to be around when some of them occur. In the meantime let us go deeper into the future with a sense of wonder.

* * * * *

Front cover: Dozmary Pool
Back cover: Author Michael Williams walking on Dartmoor

I HAVE a hunch – and hope – the twenty-first century will see a big break-through for the paranormal. Whether this will be one spectacular leap or a steady accumulation of evidence remains to be seen – maybe a combination of both. In my lifetime we have seen a vast build up of evidence: photographs, film, tape recordings, first-hand accounts from people of integrity, and, not least, improved health through healing. But we do look for one major break-through; like film of a ghost or ghosts and proof of the nature of ghosts. As a ghost hunter for thirty years I hope to be around when that moment comes.

More Bossiney Books ...

PSYCHIC PHENOMENA of the WEST
by Michael Williams
The subject of a Daphne Skinnard interview in BBC Radio Cornwall
'Michael Williams continues his well-known researches into the strange and the inexplicable . . . cases range from Cornwall to Wiltshire . . .'
The Cornish Guardian

SUPERSTITION AND FOLKLORE
by Michael Williams
A survey of Westcountry Superstitions: Interviews on the subject and some Cornish and Devon folklore.
'. . . the strictures that we all ignore at our peril. To help us keep out of trouble, Mr Williams has prepared a comprehensive list.'
Frank Kempe, North Devon Journal-Herald

STRANGE STORIES FROM DEVON
Rosemary Anne Lauder and Michael Williams. 46 photographs.
Strange shapes and places – strange characters – the man they couldn't hang, and a Salcombe mystery, the Lynmouth disaster and a mysterious house are only some of the strange stories.
'. . . full of good stories, accompanied by many photographs of local happenings which have mystified.'
Mary Richards, Tavistock Times

SUPERNATURAL IN SOMERSET
Rosemary Clinch
Atmospheres, healing, dowsing, fork-bending and strange encounters are only some of the subjects featured inside these pages. A book, destined to entertain and enlighten – one which will trigger discussion – certain to be applauded and attacked.
'. . . an illustrated study of strange encounters and extraordinary powers . . .'
Somerset County Gazette

MYSTERIES OF THE SOUTH WEST
by Tamsin Thomas of BBC Radio Cornwall
A tour of ancient sites in Cornwall and on Dartmoor.
'There is little doubt that Tamsin Thomas has become the 'Voice of Cornwall'.
Ronnie Hoyle, North Cornwall Advertiser

SOMERSET MYSTERIES
Polly Lloyd & Michael Williams

KING ARTHUR IN THE WEST
Felicity Young & Michael Williams

ABOUT EXMOOR
Polly Lloyd

CURIOSITIES OF EXMOOR
Felicity Young

SECRET DEVON
Introduced by Sarah Foot

We shall be delighted to send you our catalogue giving full details of our growing list of titles and forthcoming publications. If you have difficulty in obtaining our titles, write direct to Bossiney Books, Land's End, St Teath, Bodmin, Cornwall.